DANGEROUS GUIDE TO LEADING INNOVATION

D1466597

DANGEROUS GUIDE TO LEADING INNOVATION

How You Can Turn Your Team into an Innovation Force

Impact Innovation

Simon Gardner, Nick Fawcett, Sharron Fenemore and Phil Davis

BLOOMSBURY

First published in Great Britain 2011

Bloomsbury Publishing Plc
50 Bedford Square
London WC1B 3DP
www.bloomsbury.com

Copyright © Impact Innovation 2011

All rights reserved; no part of this publication may be reproduced, stored in a retrieval system, or transmitted by any means, electronic, mechanical, photocopying or otherwise, without the prior written permission of the Publisher.

No responsibility for loss caused to any individual or organisation acting or refraining from action as a result of the material in this publication can be accepted by the Publishers or the authors.

A CIP record for this book is available from the British Library.

ISBN: 978-1-4081-2503-8

This book is produced using paper that is made from wood grown in managed, sustainable forests. It is natural, renewable and recyclable. The logging and manufacturing processes conform to the environmental regulations of the country of origin.

Design by Fiona Pike, Pike Design, Winchester
Typeset by Saxon Graphics, Derby
Printed and bound by CPI Group (UK) Ltd, Croydon, CR0 4YY

CONTENTS

introduction

This innocent-looking book...dangerous? No?

It's true – you're not in any danger of it biting your hand off or running amok.

However, as a part of the Dangerous Series, it is dangerous in a number of other ways:

- It contains very little theory, very little management language, and very little academic gloss. We haven't done huge amounts of research into different organisations, or read vast quantities of the latest business thinking. It is clothed in very little *except* (and this is a big except) our own experience. In other words, it is standing here naked apart from its underclothes. But as you'll see from all the masses of practical stories and examples we've included, those underclothes are woven from reality – so it is not embarrassed about flaunting itself!
- The book is written in a conversational style. You might hate it, but we wanted to write as if we were talking to you, not preaching or compiling an academic thesis.
- Quite a lot of it challenges conventional thinking about both leadership and leading for innovation. There's a big danger that you won't agree with us about some of it. That's OK – so long as it provokes you to do some thinking yourself.
- Speaking of challenges, this book constantly challenges *you* to go and do, so you raise your self-awareness and build yourself as a leader. These challenges, which we've called Dangerous Quests, dare you to do things you might not have done before. And if dangerous scares you, think adventurous instead.
- We've made a lot of assumptions about what you already know and what you can do, so we haven't gone into the minutiae of telling you how to heat the water before you can have boiled eggs for breakfast. That would have resulted in an enormous, and much less interesting, book. Is it dangerous to assume that you're an intelligent reader? You decide.

OUR EXPERIENCE IS YOUR EXPERIENCE

So who are we to go writing dangerous books on leading for innovation? Maybe our client list should do the talking. We've worked with a whole host of companies, from Accor Hotels, Allied Domecq, the BBC and Britannia Building Society, right through to O2, Tesco and Waitrose. Recently we have been working with many different organisations within the NHS, helping them to harness innovation and developing their people to improve the services they offer. Many of our customers have won awards for the work they've done through being innovative and developing people who can lead for innovation at all levels of the organisation. And as a result, we've developed a number of approaches, thoughts and ideas over the last 10 years – tried and tested in real situations – that we feel are worth sharing.

We hope that you enjoy this book. We hope you enjoy trying out the things in it too. We hope you develop yourself in ways you couldn't imagine. And as a result, we hope it helps you to unleash the innovation pent up in those around you too – if, of course, they are ready for it.

Good luck!
The Impact Innovation Team

chapter 1
making the case for innovation

Just the title of this book makes it one of the most dangerous business books in the world. Why? Because it refers to two of the most overused, overrated, overburdened words in the whole business lexicon. Type 'innovation' into Google and the number of results returned has nine digits. Search for either leadership or innovation on Amazon, and you'll find tens of thousands of books with these words in the title. So are we mad?

Actually, we don't think so; we just like to live dangerously. And we have a burning desire to rescue these words from the heaps of burble and jargon into which they've fallen. So we'll start by defining what *we* mean by them:

Leadership – Contrary to popular belief, this isn't just the management style of some giant of industry or politics who strides along at the head of an army of underlings, barking commands and dreaming up brilliant strategies. Not to be confused with management (we believe, quite unfashionably, that you still need great managers in organisations too), leadership can also mean the doing of everyday things to get the best out of everyone for the success of your business. It is all the things you do and say to your team, colleagues, customers and suppliers – people stuff, continuously delivered in individual, person-sized chunks.

Innovation – Innovation is inextricably linked with creativity. Creativity, in this context, means coming up with great ideas; innovation means doing something with them to create new value. So when we talk about innovation in this book, we mean both things. You can't have innovation without creativity, but you can't create new value from creativity on its own.

WHO ARE THE GREAT LEADERS FOR INNOVATION?
When we think of innovation, some familiar names spring to mind: Richard Branson, Anita Roddick, Steve Jobs, James Dyson and

the Google guys (Larry Page and Sergey Brin). It's true that all these people are great innovators and should be worshipped and admired as such. However, some of the iconic people you naturally think about are principally great *ideas people* – not necessarily great *leaders for innovation*. The two aren't always the same thing. There are countless extraordinary ideas that would never have seen the light of day – let alone changed the world – if other people with a gift for innovation hadn't taken them up and made them real.

In order to be a good leader for innovation, you do NOT have to be very creative yourself. It's more about knowing how to foster and nurture ideas. Our friend Gary, a senior person in another organisation, is fantastic at this. He's very encouraging, asks lots of questions about our ideas, looks at ways to take them forward, comes up with suggestions for how other people can help and so on. As a consequence, whenever we think we've come up with a good idea, the first person we tell – and look forward to telling – is Gary. Almost immediately it becomes more real, one step nearer to becoming something concrete, simply thanks to his attitude. In other words, the great leaders for innovation often aren't the ones who become famous. They are people with open minds, who understand innovation themselves and know how to draw it out in others.

Bullish isn't always best when it comes to leadership (it can be a bit too close to bullshit, actually). If you're not a gung ho sort of person with lots of ideas, don't worry – you can still be a great leader for innovation.

Just learning to curb that initial reaction of 'I'm not sure if it'll work' can take you much of the way there. To help you with the changes you'll need to make, we've come up with some Dangerous Quests for you to tackle. They're an important part of you becoming what you want to be.

dangerous quest

Focus properly on getting the best out of the people around you, and the big things (top-line strategies, bottom-line profitability etc.) will fall naturally into place.

SO WHAT'S THIS BOOK ABOUT?

There are lots of good books on structuring organisations to make people more creative, setting up innovation processes or creating high-level innovation strategies. In fact we might be writing a Dangerous book on this soon. But the book you're holding isn't like that – it's about *you*. It's not about the organisation, it's personal. You don't have to worry about structures, or processes or changing the whole company behemoth; you only have to worry about yourself. It's about how *you* can lead and manage and encourage the people around you to be more creative and innovative. So stop worrying about how you haven't got 'idea hotspots', or 'rapid innovation sessions' or 'innovation rooms' full of bean bags, stress balls and table football games, and get on with being innovative in the areas you can control.

In this book, you'll find a complete innovation leadership kit to help you. Take on some of the Dangerous Quests, grab a few of the fun and practical tools, change your innovation beliefs and behaviours and you too will have people around you buzzing with great ideas – not mad, random, off-the-wall ones, but ideas that are great in the real sense: insightful, thought-provoking, thought through, and of the right level and scale. You and your people will be implementing more of these great ideas as well, to the benefit of your business. And, not least, you will become the team and the leader with the reputation for innovation in your organisation.

Have you ever found yourself thinking any of the following?

- Why do we always do things the same way?
- Why is it always me who has to think of the ideas round here?
- Why can't my team/colleagues be more creative?
- We either get mad ideas or sad ideas – never the right idea.
- Actually we're not bad at the ideas bit, but when it comes to implementation ...
- Everyone moans that we aren't innovative as an organisation, but no one does anything about it.

If so, this is the book for you. We've even written it in a different way, each member of the team contributing individual chapters before letting each other add and amend. It means we've each had a say and built on each others' ideas (more of that later). It also means that rather than being constrained by an expectation to sound the same, we've expressed ourselves in different ways throughout the book. In the context of leadership for innovation, giving people room to be themselves is important.

MAKING THE CASE TO BECOME A LEADER FOR INNOVATION

As we said in the introduction, this book is not going to tell you how to reorganise your whole company so that you are better at innovating new products or services. Sorry, we know that is probably what you would like to happen. This very big challenge is for another day. We are deliberately starting where you can make a difference.

Trust us, designing and implementing organisational change, redesigning processes and creating structural improvement are very big and time-consuming exercises. We know from personal experience. Yes, it does make a difference – but so can you, now, in the organisation structure you are in, with the processes you have (although you might need to tweak some of them) and with the team that sits around you.

But what if you're not a senior executive who spends their days deciding on new markets, new products or new growth strategies? What influence can you have on how innovative your business is and what new things you need to be doing? What if you feel like a relatively small cog in a huge machine?

We believe you are in the perfect place to really make innovation happen, and there are lots of reasons for this.

Big improvement projects can be great but let's look at the facts – 70 per cent of change projects fail to deliver the improvement expected – many fail altogether and never get implemented. Smaller, frequent and incremental change is far more likely to succeed.

Big programmes often focus on structures and processes, which are important, but it is very often individuals' behaviour that is key to being more innovative and doing things differently. This is the very thing that you can change more effectively in a smaller team (and it is often behaviours that the big initiatives forget to include).

In order to deliver new products and services, you need an organisation where every department, team and individual is looking to improve what they do. That's why we believe there is a stronger case for small scale, team-based innovation than big scale change.

INTERNAL AND EXTERNAL INNOVATION

Innovation can be applied to two key areas, each needing innovation leadership:

Internal – With your colleagues, you can do things cheaper, faster, more simply, effectively, smoothly, once only, or not at all. So if you're sitting in finance, HR, training or communications, this is for you.

External – Customers want new products and services, they want better and cheaper ways to do business with you – they want, they want. So if you're sitting in marketing, sales or product development, it is obvious who is demanding the innovation and why.

But hold on. Isn't this all just about business improvement? That may be true, but if your business improvement is also about doing things differently, then we believe that you can be better at improving your business if you approach it with an innovation and creativity hat on.

This book is about giving you as the leader of your team the capability to approach the improvement of your area, of your organisation, with innovation as your weapon of choice.

What about other great improvement methods: Lean, Kaizen, Quality Circles etc.? Whatever you do, do not abandon any of them: they are all great. But putting innovative and creative thinking into the way that you go about improving your department's performance will make these methods even more effective.

So, what if you need to improve the effectiveness of your training? Of course, look at eliminating waste, taking out what doesn't add value, removing duplication. But also ask yourself the following questions.

* What if we did no training at all?
* Who else has solved this problem, and can we go and see them?
* What if there were five minutes of training every day (no big sessions offsite)?
* What are we fundamentally trying to achieve with this training?
* What is the complete learning cycle and how can we affect it in different ways?

This book will help you and your team ask some different questions and, more importantly, create some different solutions to improve performance in different ways. That's the focus for the book – it's all about:

- your beliefs, behaviours, capability and skills;
- unlocking your own creativity;
- unlocking the creativity of your teams;
- innovation in your team or department, and its role within your organisation.

It will be about you cutting your innovation leadership teeth on relatively small stuff to start with, working with your team to do things in better and different ways.

And there are some other things for free...Remember we said that 70 per cent of big improvement initiatives fail? Well, that's often *not* because the new solution and its structures and processes weren't the right ones. It is because those making the change failed to engage people in the organisation in such a way that they wanted to adopt, use and follow new ways of doing things. As the diagram below illustrates improvement is fundamentally only about doing two things. The first is designing and implementing the new Thing – process product, service etc. and the second is the engagement of the people so that they embrace the change.

Improvement is about just two things

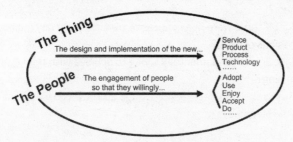

What's great about using innovation as your approach, as shown in the illustration above, is that you can just as readily apply it to the way you engage your colleagues so that they love what your team are proposing, just as much as to the 'thing' you are developing and implementing. This book includes some creative ways to implement the change so that, rather than resisting and ignoring it, people love it and want it. So, let's get on with it.

WORD CLOUDS

For each chapter, we have created a small word cloud (using Wordle.Net, a free word cloud generator from the Internet) to help summarise the main points and topics of conversation. We hope you find them thought provoking.

chapter 2

you're more innovative than you think

There are many types of innovator. There are many types of innovation. Innovation doesn't have to be about the eureka moment, or boldly going where no man has gone before. It can be just this: doing simple everyday things, differently. Consider this great change quote from Albert Einstein:

'Insanity is doing the same things over and over again and expecting different results.'

It applies to the struggle many organisations have with innovation and explains why they end up in the same place time after time. They keep doing the same things, in exactly the same way. To end up in a different place, you need to start in a different way, follow a different path or at least do one or two things differently.

HAVE I GOT WHAT IT TAKES TO BE A LEADER FOR INNOVATION?

As we start this chapter we want you to do a little bit of self-reflection by going back to those questions we mentioned in Chapter 1. This will help us work out if you are ready to start the journey and, if not, what's stopping you. Start by looking back over the last 12 months or so and answer the following questions:

- Where do all the ideas in your team/department/organisation come from?
- How often do you and/or your team spend time thinking about new ideas together?
- When did you last actively encourage your team or colleagues to do things differently and come up with some new ideas?
- And finally, how do you respond when others bring you new ideas and suggest new ways of doing things?

So, be honest. Have you ever caught yourself thinking (or even saying) any of the following?

- 'My team aren't creative.'
- 'We never have any new ideas.'
- 'I'm the one with all the ideas.'

Or worse:

- 'I have to come up with all the new ideas.'
- 'That won't work.'
- 'We've tried it before.'
- 'It works perfectly well at the moment, so why change?'

If the answer is yes to any or all of these questions, then *you* just might be the blocker of innovation in your team. Yes, YOU.

But don't despair just yet. By admitting that it might be you and that you just might need to do, or be, something different, you have made the first step towards becoming a better leader of innovation. It's that easy. If you read the whole of this book and follow just a few of the suggestions, becoming a great innovation leader is well within your grasp.

Great innovation myths #1: Genius

Talk about great innovators and many people will conjure up an image of an Einstein-like professor or even the Doc Brown character from the *Back to the Future* movies: an eccentric character, holed up in a shed that's full of drawings, half-finished projects and experiments. The innovator as inventor. But this is only one type of innovator and we would argue not the most common or the most successful.

We strongly believe innovation is NOT about the lone genius having the eureka moment. It is about ordinary people, like you and me, having an open mind to just about everything they see, hear and do. You certainly don't need to be a genius to be a great innovator, and you certainly don't need to work alone. But, to be a great innovator you do need to be a great leader – an expert in collaborating with others to get the best out of everyone.

Most importantly great leaders of innovation are experts at creating a vision and driving their team towards it. They encourage and borrow ideas from others, share those ideas and build on them, supporting, motivating and guiding their team to succeed. Here's one person's story about the impact that a lack of innovation leadership can have:

> *For many years I worked for a major high street bank in one of their retail product management teams. It was our team's responsibility to manage the portfolio of savings products, develop and launch new products, enhance existing products, set pricing and to market the entire range to our customers. We thought we were the best and most innovative product management team in the company. But looking back, I'm really not so sure. We were good, BUT knowing what I know now, we weren't great. Why? Because we weren't open to ideas from others, we didn't encourage or welcome ideas from outside our team and certainly not from branch staff.*
>
> *One of the first jobs I was given as the new marketing assistant (the lowest position in the product management team) was to go through the suggestions submitted via an ideas scheme by branch staff (the people who served our customers face to face, every single day; the receivers of direct feedback about our products and services). I can remember thinking: 'It's my first day, how will I know if the ideas are any good, perhaps they have been submitted before, what criteria should I use to assess them?' I asked my manager and to this day I can still remember her response: 'Don't worry about it; the ideas are never any good and besides, we have more than enough ideas of our own. Just send one of the standard letters in the file and they'll get a pen as a reward for sending something in.'*

> *Half the time we didn't even bother to read the submissions thoroughly and we certainly didn't enter into any dialogue with the staff to get a better understanding of the customer insight that had led to the idea in the first place. I'm afraid to say that at the time, I wasn't brave enough to challenge this outrageous behaviour and at times was probably guilty myself of 'not invented here' syndrome, adopting and following the culture being set by so called 'innovation leaders'.*

Great leaders for innovation can and do have ideas of their own, but they certainly shouldn't believe that ideas are their or even their team's sole responsibility. Equally, there are many others who use a lack of belief in their own creativity or an aversion to blank sheets of paper as excuses to avoid doing anything differently.

At Impact we have an unwavering belief that everyone can be creative in their own way. Some people just need a bit of help to bring out their creative streak or to recognise it in themselves.

a little example:

One project we ran involved working with a fantastic bunch of people from a famous retailer. Our challenge was to help them apply creativity in the development of a specific system in their organisation designed to support a set of key roles. At the beginning of this chapter we talked about the need to do things differently to end up in a different place. This is exactly what we did with this team. However, before we could get them to start in a different place, we had to convince them all that they could be creative. Eighty per cent of the group were adamant that they weren't.

Armed with plenty of optimism, our belief that everyone can be creative in their own way, and a few activities designed to unlock that creativity, we ran our first session. Using the 'try something different' approach, we started with a simple game called Paper Chains. Splitting the group into small teams of four or five, we gave each a pack of coloured paper, one pair of scissors, a roll of tape and a glue stick, and challenged them to make the longest paper chain possible in five minutes. We gave no instructions about what sort of paper chain to make, what it should look like or how it should be constructed. Within minutes, we had colourful, beautifully made paper chains adorning the tables and chairs. When we laid them all out, we had a clear winner. Admittedly, that chain wasn't quite as pretty or beautifully made as the rest, but it did constitute a chain and was certainly the longest. This quickly led to some heated debate, claims of cheating and challenging conversations about the definition of a paper chain. The winning team definitely hadn't cheated; they had thought differently and creatively about what they had been asked to do. They had started in a different place. They had chosen to make something that was still a chain of paper but rather less traditional in design. It's amazing what a simple task and a bit of healthy competition can achieve. To finish the exercise we asked everyone to try again.

The result was paper chains of all shapes and sizes, all of which were considerably longer than their first attempts. Without exception, the doubters had all been creative.

CAN I LEAD OTHERS TO BE MORE INNOVATIVE?

We have established that everyone can be creative in their own way, and you have made the first steps to recognising that you may need to change in order to be a great leader for innovation. So the next step is to understand what you actually need to do, to lead others to be more innovative. We said earlier that your role is not about having all the ideas, blocking others' ideas or doing the same things over and over again. What is it about then?

One crucial element of being a leader for innovation is to create the right environment for innovation: to understand all of the skills needed and to use the people around you, and their strengths, to make it happen.

Great innovation myths #2: You need to be famous to be a great leader for innovation

A myth that we at Impact are keen to dispel is the need to be famous to be a great leader for innovation. This clearly isn't true and here are just a few reasons why.

Was Einstein famous *before* he came up with the theory of relativity or *because* he did? Bill Gates was a self-confessed geek when he started Microsoft and Steve Jobs was a college dropout before he launched Apple Computers from his garage with his friend Steve Wozniak in 1976. Fame and wealth may come as a result of innovation, but often they are not the initial drivers. These guys didn't set out to be famous, but they did set out to make a difference and were truly passionate about their chosen paths.

About innovation, Steve Jobs said: 'Innovation distinguishes between a leader and a follower.' Commenting in the American press, one journalist wrote: 'If there has been a theme to Jobs' success it has been his genius, as it were, for finding other geniuses and promoting their brilliance.' This endorses wholeheartedly our theory on the role of a great leader:

> **Great leaders for innovation are often experts at creating the vision and driving their team towards it, encouraging ideas from others, building on ideas, at times borrowing ideas or approaches to solving problems, sharing ideas, and supporting, motivating and guiding their teams to succeed.**

To further demonstrate the point, there are many innovative companies and brands whose leaders aren't so famous.

For example, have you ever heard of Jeffrey P Bezos? Well, he founded Amazon. Howard Schultz? He is the CEO of Starbucks. Richard Reed, Jon Wright and Adam Bolan? They could be members of the latest boy band but are in fact the co-founders of the Innocent drinks brand. These guys started making smoothies in 1999 and on that first day they sold 24 bottles, and now they sell over two million a week.

Alan Yau founded Wagamama, opening his first restaurant in 1992. Gérard Basset was one of the co-founders of Hotel du Vin, which is an award-winning niche hotel chain alongside its sister company Malmaison. Both are credited with spotting a niche in a market and stepping out of the mainstream to develop a new, innovative offering. In Germany, there is a community of innovative organisations which have stood the test of time and have even been credited with helping Germany fight the recession head on. They develop high quality components that are present in a variety of everyday and high performance products, and in some cases, products that occupy niche markets. These companies, called the Mittelstand, are all small- to medium-sized companies run by serial innovators. Micom is one. Its equipment was famously used in the rescue of the Chilean miners. Micom's leader is Juergens Tinkerers, whose philosophy is to keep innovating, keep developing, and keep improving. It's a philosophy they all seem to share.

Mario Guevara is the CEO of BIC, the company behind Bic Razors, Bic Pens and other household names such as Tipp-Ex (the saviour of most students before the advent of computers). Famously in 2008, it also launched a 'no frills', just-talk mobile phone, stretching its brand to the budget end of the mobile communications industry.

One of India's celebrated innovators is Shiv Nadar. At a time when India only had 250 computers, he saw the opportunity and founded a technology company called HCL. This company is now recognised by many commentators as one to watch in the global IT systems and outsourcing market.

The last person we'll talk about here is not famous, is not the CEO of a big corporation, and doesn't have a glamorous job. She came from humble beginnings and is a person who has a real passion for change. She is committed to making a difference in one of the most difficult environments we can think of: the NHS. Our friend Lynne began life as a nurse (although she says she still is one), and from day one was absolutely determined to make the NHS a more innovative place. She left nursing practice and went to learn about innovation from everybody she could – agencies, academics, practitioners, as well as pioneers in the NHS. Lynne is exactly the sort of person we believe you can be. Through her sheer passion, determination and great leadership skills, which have grown over time, Lynne has developed countless frontline tools, techniques and methodologies. Through a practitioners network she has made a real difference not only to the NHS but also to the millions of patients it serves.

THE TRAITS OF LEADERSHIP

Just for a moment, let's pause and think about the leaders we've talked about. They are very different but they have traits that define them and make them the leaders they are. There are three levels to these traits:

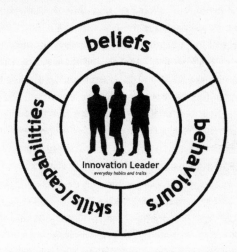

Beliefs – The ideals they aspire to and hold true to in every adventure they embark on. In terms of innovation leadership, these beliefs help to underpin how they view the world with respect to innovation.

Behaviours – A core set of 'conscious' innovation-led behaviours that they exhibit when they undertake challenges, activities and tasks.

Capabilities – A specific set of innovation-orientated capabilities (but by no means exclusive to innovation), which enable them to undertake challenges, activities and tasks to achieve their goals as leaders for innovation.

BUILDING YOUR OWN INNOVATION LEADERSHIP WHEEL

It's important that you really think about your personal Innovation Leadership Wheel as it will help you define what you are about, and where you need to develop and grow. But at the moment we just want you to think about beliefs; this is key to getting your ambition defined. You can populate the behaviours and capabilities as you progress through this book.

Cast your eye back over the innovation leaders we have referred to already in this chapter, and think about others who personally inspire you (they can be from any walk of life but they must stand out as leaders of innovation). If you can, find pictures of them to help you visualise who they are. Now think about what beliefs these leaders have that have made them stand out and with which you can associate. For example, if we were doing this for Superman, we might identify his beliefs as *bringing out the good in everybody, everywhere*, or, *people want peace and justice*.

Using this as provocation, ask yourself: as a leader for innovation, what do I believe? In innovation terms, a belief might be: *everybody can be innovative in their own way*. Or, *through innovation, we can bring about change*.

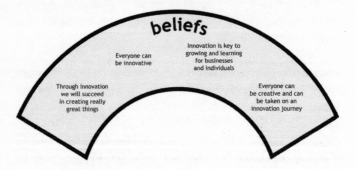

The key here is not to create an exhaustive list. It's to get five or so really clean and crisp beliefs with which you can strongly identify. Don't read any further until you've done this. It's important that you are able to test your beliefs as you read on.

We won't keep referring to this wheel, asking you to complete this and that, because that won't work for you. Consider it more a tool you can use to help shape your learning as you go – you are becoming a leader for innovation after all, and each experience will be unique to you and your situation. So feel free to capture them on your own developing version of the wheel. Trust us, you'll find it quite rewarding to see the picture build.

Great innovation myths #3: The innovation switch

It's clear you can't do this overnight. Innovation is not a switch on the side of your head. But what you can do is create a wave of innovation that runs first through you and then through your team, colleagues and beyond. The rest of the book is devoted to helping you create this wave of innovation. It starts with you, but it will end with everybody joining in.

So, before we close this chapter we want you to do one other thing. Check out a clip on YouTube – just type in 'First Follower' and look for the clip called Leadership Lessons from Dancing Guy. Watch it, enjoy it, laugh and then watch it again and again – it moves at real pace so you will have to pay attention. And make sure to listen and think about the commentary. It will give you a sense of what your journey towards becoming a great leader for innovation may look and feel like.

key learning points

- Recognising you may need to change, from being the person with all the ideas to a helper and supporter of people with their own ideas, is your first act in starting the journey towards leadership.
- You don't need to be famous or godlike to be a leader for innovation – in fact, quite the reverse might be true.
- A leader for innovation is not an island, a lone genius or a mad inventor.

Thinking about your own set of core beliefs is a critical step in shaping what you are about as a leader for innovation. It will help you think about how you view life as a leader, stay true to yourself especially in times of adversity and develop the behaviours and capabilities you need to succeed.

WORD CLOUD

chapter 3
getting in the zone

o did you watch the clip? You need to, because leadership is about stepping up and making a start. There's no need to learn the dance moves, though...*that was just a plus!*

WHAT CAN YOU DO TO GET YOURSELF IN THE PERSONAL INNOVATION ZONE?

We've already established that everyone can be innovative, and if you're still in doubt whether 'everyone' includes you, this chapter should get you into the right place. And remember the Innovation Leadership Wheel as we start to explore behaviours that will help you fly.

If you want to kick-start innovation in your organisation, you need to start *feeling* innovative in yourself. But how do you feel innovative or creative if you still don't believe you are? And if you do believe, how can you turn that into positive action?

There's a simple answer:

> **You have the power to choose to be innovative, and once you are in control of that choice there'll be no stopping you.**

Imagine if you could use all the things you already do in normal life as tools to make yourself more creative, and at the same time signal to your team and colleagues (and customers) that you mean business when it comes to being creative and inspiring innovation. Imagine you could grow as an individual too.

It's one of those things in life that is simple but not easy. Choosing to be innovative takes practice, focus and, dare we say, a little bit of self-understanding. This chapter is all about helping you to step consciously into your own personal innovation zone.

dangerous quest

To kick-start your own innovation journey, start your day by doing something differently: wear something unusual (perhaps a pink shirt, loud tie, a dress rather than trousers, gel your hair...) and note the response from those around you. Take a different route to work, park in a different place, use public transport or walk part of the way and keep your eyes peeled for inspiration. Who knows, you may just find a quicker way, learn something new or spot something you didn't know was there. If you are feeling brave, inspire your team or colleagues to start thinking differently by getting them to try this too.

WHO WILL BELL THE CAT?

There is one key behaviour that is inextricably linked with getting into your zone of innovation: courage. It may seem odd to label creativity and innovation as courageous, but to be a true leader for innovation you need to be the one who is willing to take a few risks and even suffer failure. You need to be the one who demonstrates to the people around you, in words and actions, that it's okay to come up with and talk about new ideas, however ridiculous. That may mean you are the one who gets shot down a few times, but if you do it on your own terms and in the right way you'll set the right levels of permission for those around you.

There's an idiom which has fallen out of use in recent years: who will bell the cat? It means who will take on a courageous act, and its origin is a 13th-century fable. A group of mice were being terrorised by a nasty feline and so one brave young mouse suggested an idea – they should tie a bell around the neck of the cat so they could always hear him coming. All the mice thought that this was a splendid brainwave until the oldest of all the mice piped up: 'It's a good idea but who will bell the cat?'

If you are really going to make innovative change happen, at some point you are going to have to bell the cat.

dangerous quest

Spend a few minutes writing down the tasks for this week about which you are feeling slightly apprehensive (it's OK, no one's looking). You know the kind of thing: that difficult phone call, presenting to the board, making polite conversation over dinner – we all have our own list.

Imagine a red line standing between you and achieving one of the items on your list. Now, every time you tick off one of the items this week imagine you are stepping over the red line. We'll check back to see how you've done later in this chapter.

PUTTING IT INTO PRACTICE

A friend of ours loves this technique. After 12 years of working for the same large blue chip company he decided to Houdini his way out of the golden handcuffs and take a couple of years off to travel the world and find himself.

He popped in to see us when he got back, on the premise of wanting to talk business, but in reality just to brag about where he'd been. We asked him about any culture shock he'd experienced whilst exploring exotic locations like Cambodia, Columbia, Calcutta and places which began with other letters too. Expecting tales of eating fruit bat curry (like chicken, apparently) whilst dancing a Peruvian tango (like Argentinean, apparently), his reply took us rather by surprise.

It was in his local Tesco, whilst stocking up on provisions after returning to the UK. In fact, arriving home for him was the biggest of all culture shocks.

As he settled back into normal life he realised the need to make some money and managed to land an exciting job as Sales Director in a leading creative agency. He was, quite understandably, pretty nervous after more than two years out of the corporate world. How was he going to be this cutting edge innovation-meister when he felt that his knowledge and confidence were lacking?

He did two things in the three weeks before he started the job to get back into feeling innovative. Firstly, like our little challenge above, he wrote down all the things (big and small) that he felt worried about and thought might be quite stretching when he was in his new role. He then equated each of these to something that he felt the same about in his current world. I asked him for a few examples.

He knew in his Sales Director role he would have to:

- get his team together every morning and inspire them to do their best throughout the day;
- make cold calls to senior business people to open doors for his sales team;
- be proficient in new IT systems and, simply;
- meet new people, be liked and be interesting.

To prepare himself for these new challenges he:

- started coaching the local youth football team;
- made a list of his long lost relatives, tracked them down and called one of them each day. He even started calling up live debate shows on BBC Radio 5 Live;
- met up with an old colleague and helped him with creating a new business case, supporting budget and a presentation to the board;
- signed up for as many singles nights as he could find (being single...).

By doing all these things he boosted his capability, his knowledge and importantly his belief that he could be innovative even when he was feeling nervous and under pressure. He also re-immersed himself in all his travelling experiences by looking at photos and caressing mementos, trying to remember what he did every day, even what he had to eat for dinner each and every night.

After all this reflection he realised he had experienced more creative stimulus over the preceding couple of years than many people experience in their entire lives. He then started thinking about the ideas that these experiences gave him and felt invigorated by the armoury of stories, new concepts and different perspectives that he now had at his disposal. Literally, it was new energy for innovation.

Needless to say he went on to be immensely successful and a true innovation leader from day one.

TOP TIPS FOR GETTING INTO THE ZONE

We've so far seen just a couple of techniques. After extensive research with our clients we've identified our top 11 tips (why be limited to 10?) to get you into your innovation zone, and sprinkled them with firsthand stories from people we know. In the spirit of this book these tips get more dangerous the further down the list you go. Pick a place to start and then give them a try. If you're really committed, do them all.

1. Rip up the sub-routine

2. Think small

3. Once you grow up, you can't grow down

4. Don't mind your language

5. Life's an adventure

6. You don't always get a stupid answer

7. Roll with it

8. Make a new friend

9. Say hello and don't blush

10. Get a bug

11. Just a little white lie

1. Rip up the sub-routine

If you don't do anything else, do this! One of the biggest blockers to innovative behaviour is the way we as human beings get locked into not just the routines, but the sub-routines of everyday life.

The problem is most of us strive all our lives to get into simple routines that allows us to negotiate successfully all the outside forces we experience, but unfortunately these little routines are the bane of creative behaviour. We're obviously not saying that routine is bad, and we're great advocates of not fixing what isn't broken, but mixing it up a little bit will make a huge difference to how you (ahem) stimulate yourself, creatively.

Have a think about the routines and sub-routines you follow every single day, when you arrive in the office, pull out your laptop, switch it on, go and make a cup of coffee while it's booting up, ask how Jean's weekend was and say yours was fine, sit down again, check your emails, flick to Facebook (protocols permitting of course)...You know how it is.

Even before you've reached that point you will have followed at least 50 routines since you woke up and got out of that side of bed this morning (trust us, we've done the research). So tomorrow, try brushing your teeth after you've had a shower, making your cup of tea in a mug and driving to work on the country roads instead of the motorway.

On that last one, we recently ran a creative workshop with some leaders from a leading supermarket chain in the UK. The venue was a small pub/country hotel about 10 miles from their head office, a regular meeting place for them. To prime their internal innovation engines we asked them to drive from their houses to the venue via a completely new route.

This simple act inspired some fascinating results. Some people arrived much sooner than they had anticipated and were delighted, a few were late and were frustrated, some people were arguing about the quickest possible route, other people planned their weekend based on new places they'd spotted, locals were lecturing on nearby road developments in the last 20 years, some people just couldn't bring themselves to do it (exhibiting a possible fear of the unknown), some used it to spark a new routine and so on.

All were, however, energised and ready to tackle the big (and complicated) creative challenge that lay ahead that day. Without a doubt it would have taken us an hour or two to inspire that type of enthusiasm in the same old venue. They walked in the door ready to go.

2. Think small
In the 21st century we want everything now: a nanosecond's unwanted wait for your favourite news website to load can cause a sudden and uncontrollable fit of rage and swift navigation elsewhere.

Quite understandably, we expect to make change happen immediately so we're always searching for the big thing to meet that need. In fact it's the little things, the things you might not even notice, that can make a huge difference.

Try buying some outrageously colourful socks.

A colleague of ours tells a story about the bright socks he wears whenever he flies. Going though security these days is one of the most stressful and annoying things you can do, and the security guards often have a thankless task in making sure they have every base covered. So having observed this situation he wondered how he could brighten up the mood? So now, when the security guard asks him to remove his shoes to go through the x-ray scanner, he does so with aplomb and delight. He usually gets a welcome smile from said member of staff but also sets off some fun banter with the other travellers in the line. He is transformed into a leader of this transitory group in a matter of seconds.

After hearing that story, a member of the team went out and bought a massive variety pack of brightly coloured socks. Every single morning he puts a pair on and it makes him feel like someone who is not afraid to laugh at himself. He says that feeling like that every morning gets him into the right mindset to be creative.

So don't just go off and buy some socks, think about the impact of the socks on the situation. What little things can you change to make you feel like that?

3. Once you grow up you can't grow down

It's an old cliché in the world of creativity and innovation, to put yourself in the shoes of a five-year-old child and think about how they would solve a problem. Not only is it easier said than done, it requires very small feet.

There is of course much to learn from this technique; the trick is how you actually do it. Rather than getting into any five-year-old child's shoes, get into your own. Try thinking back to your childhood days; picture a time when you were playing a game or building something. Imagine we're having a great time building a garage out of Lego®. What emotions are we going through? Excitement, real focus, a bit of frustration, control, a belief in what we're creating and pride, to name a few. Now, staying in that frame of mind it's easy to think of pretty radical solutions to problems, however simple or complex they may be. We employ this technique every time we come home from IKEA ... don't we?

Just remember you don't have to be an adult all the time.

4. Don't mind your language

We're not advocating swearing here but we think throwing in a bit of different language can really spark something.

If I talk the language of innovation with purpose, am I actually being more innovative? This chapter is all about feeling innovative so it's a good step – if people think you're sounding more innovative (or you think they do) you are on the right track.

Try using words and phrases that encourage creative energy. Do what works for you and change your stock phrases. Forget saying things like we need to be more innovative (what is someone supposed to do with that?), or let's make it impactful (who made that word up anyway?).

In a previous life one of us used to stack shelves in a large supermarket. His job every fourth Wednesday of the month was to reconfigure the ends of each aisle with new promotions – usually sponsored by Coke, Heinz and the like (in case you wanted to know, they're cleverly called promotion ends). Every month his manager told him to make his 'ends' as impactful as possible. Armed with a set of plan-o-grams (you're learning some top retail terms now) and a stack of products, he always strived to make an impact, only for his manager to return hours later and inform him that it wasn't impactful enough. Try harder. What do you want me to do, he would think, stand the Coke bottles on their end? Eventually he came to the realisation that his manager didn't have a clue what he was after either and worked out what he needed to do himself.

Our budding shelf-stacker must have done something right, as in a couple of years he ended up managing his own store. He made a point of never uttering the 'i' word, instead he would use creative words and language. This made sure his team knew what they were doing and reassured him that he was influencing them in the right direction. The key to being really successful at this, of course, is to know your people so you can inspire them in a way that is right for them.

He would get them to imagine they were building a house, painting a masterpiece, writing a song, fixing a computer, whatever turned them on. Then they imagined their 'end' was a billboard in Times Square or Piccadilly Circus. They were creating works of art, an ultimate advertisement and window to an exciting new world. It sounds corny but his people delivered nothing but superbly striking displays, simply because he spoke the language of innovation in a way that every individual could relate to in their own particular way.

Try it out; you might just turn your next little project into a work of art.

5. Life's an adventure

It so is. If you are bored, or think you are, you will always struggle to be a leader for innovation. If you are jaded, get more adventure in your life. And that adventure can appear in the most unpromising places:

I recently decided to learn how to cook Chinese food and in my infinite wisdom thought I'd try something 'simple' like spring rolls. It does sound simple but the array of ingredients in those tasty little suckers is amazing.

I spent a day exploring the back streets of Birmingham trying to buy all those ingredients and what an adventure it was. Of course you can buy a few of the bits and bobs you need in Waitrose, but the majority is pretty specialist. So, after a day of searching and finding and learning lots of new food types I'd never heard of, I went home to make my little rolls.

> *I couldn't believe how creative the process could be! Big ones, little ones, fat ones, thin ones. I felt an amazing sense of pride and satisfaction. I even took a picture of them they were so cool!*
>
> *That little decision to search out goodies and to make something new reignited my excitement and confidence that you can teach an old dog new tricks.*

A friend came back from holiday and decided that there was too much excitement on his doorstep. Instead of buying the Lonely Planet Guide to Marrakech, he went for the British edition instead. Every weekend he goes on a mini-adventure round the UK. He even uses it when he's travelling on business during the week.

Why not make every opportunity an adventure? If you want something in between shopping and scooting off round the country, try exploring your town on an open top bus. You've probably been thinking about doing it for years. Don't wait; do it today.

6. You don't always get a stupid answer

How many times have you bitten your lip, out of fear of looking stupid, and not asked a question? How many times have you done that only for someone else to ask the same question and get a totally rational answer and a bit of praise for their interest and inquisitiveness?

> *Whilst working for a consultancy firm I recall being in a typically feisty cross-directorate meeting. It was generally (as I saw it) a high stakes, testosterone-fuelled, bun fight that bred behaviour I didn't like.*
>
> *In this particular meeting the commercial director asked for people to raise their hands if they didn't know the*

> *meaning of the economics phrase 'Average Propensity to Consume', which appeared in a report he was reading. I had no idea. However, suspecting that admitting such a gap in my business knowledge would surely be a career-limiting move I kept still, with a poker face of fake wisdom.*
>
> *A few hands were raised by the proverbial lambs to the slaughter and I sat back smugly, amazed at their stupidity. The commercial director looked around the room with venom and aggressively exclaimed, 'I ain't got a (expletive deleted) clue either.' He pointed in my general direction and said, 'Come on then, Sonny, explain to us all what it's about then.' Smugness quashed, who was the stupid one now? I went on to make up a story about household statistical analysis and the likelihood to eat cream cakes. It didn't go well.*

(If you're interested, 'Average Propensity to Consume' is actually the percentage of income people want to spend. Simple, when you know the answer. Shame they don't say it like that.)

Our advice is, always ask the stupid question. See it as learning, filling in the gaps rather than exposing them. The chances are if you don't know the answer, the majority of people won't either.

7. Roll with it

There is a cult 1970s book called *The Dice Man*, written by George Cockcroft under the guise of his alter ego Luke Rhinehart. It starts off well and then tails off in a rather twisted way, but the concept is great. The main character gives over his decision-making process to the roll of a dice. *If it's a six I have a day off work today; if it's below three I'll buy a gun.* You get the gist.

It's dangerous, yes, but a useful little technique. When someone asks you if you'd like to do something, note your internal reaction and then go with the opposite.

> Last Saturday night I was asked if I would like to go the ballet. My internal response was screaming at me, 'NO...it's boring and you'll hate it'. I said yes and had a wonderful time, making a few new friends along the way.

8. Make a new friend

This may not sound all that dangerous, but it's something that gets harder and harder to do as we get older. We become less tolerant and more set in our ways. However, think of all the benefits. Who are the people to whom you can say anything? Who are the people with whom you can discuss your secret passions and wildest dreams? Yes, it's your mates. To make a new friend is a creative act.

I recently moved to a brand new town where I knew absolutely no one. It's just like starting a new job apart from the fact that if you don't want to, you don't have to speak to anyone at all. In the first two months I met no one at all and my creativity went backwards. Having no one to bounce silly ideas off meant having no one with whom I could discuss how to fix the state of the world or how to get players to be more creative on the football pitch.

So, on realising my slip I set myself a simple creative challenge: make a friend in every pub. (Obviously, you can insert a different location to suit your own preferences: each piece of equipment in the gym, every café, each section of the library, each bench in the park, etc.)

I spent a very pleasant Saturday afternoon, and evening, and night talking to whoever ended up directly next to me in the pub I happened to be in at the time. Needless to say you don't hit the friendship jackpot every time, but since that *day I have two new close friends with whom I can express my creative thoughts.*

Yes, it took a bit of courage to get going, and it got a bit hairy in places, but the thrill of meeting new people, listening to their stories and being inspired by their brand new perspectives on life led to numerous new ideas back at work the following Monday morning.

9. Say hello and don't blush

So what stops us stepping over the creative line: fear of looking stupid, social conformity? Try saying 'hello' to everyone you pass for a whole day. How does it make you feel? Uncomfortable?

We were working in a large inner city hospital recently and were discussing the power of ideas with frontline staff. An operating theatre assistant quite understandably made the point that it was difficult to put forward ideas when their work colleagues (especially doctors) wouldn't even respond when they said 'hello' in the morning. If this simple act of not responding was stifling their creativity, we asked them what they thought they could do about it.

Amongst many other ideas, they suggested they should have a Say Hello crusade. Starting the following morning they all made sure they made contact with every single person by making eye contact and saying 'hello'. They made a pact to keep going until everyone would respond with an equally cordial 'hello'.

After a few weeks the results where amazing. Not only was there a raised level of conversation and team connectivity, but with a simple 'hello' all staff were allowed to be more creative, air their ideas and more importantly see some results from their suggestions.

It's the power of hello. Try it out for yourself, say 'hello' to everyone you pass (within reason) on your way to work tomorrow. After the first three or four people you'll stop feeling quite so embarrassed and the pinkness in your cheeks will slowly diminish. By the end of your commute you will feel liberated by the power of connecting with people, without the fear of looking stupid. You'll even find by the next day that you'll see a few of the same people and they'll be the ones making eye contact and saying 'hello'.

10. Get a bug

There's an amusing exchange in an episode of the hit US comedy *Friends* where Joey philosophises about the power of facing your fears to get over commitment issues. It goes like this:

> **Joey:** Face your fear. You have a fear of heights? You go to the top of the building. You're afraid of bugs? Get a bug, right? In this case, you have a fear of commitment. So I say you go in there and be the most committed guy there ever was. Go for it, man. Jump off the high dive. Stare down the barrel of a gun, pee into the wind.
>
> **Chandler:** Yeah. Joe, I assure you if I'm staring down the barrel of a gun, I'm gonna be pretty much peeing every which way.

So, what *is* your fear of being a leader for innovation? Is it that you won't have all the ideas? You might not be inspiring enough? You might start an uncontrollable torrent of creativity around you?

Take a minute to think about what is it is and then work out how you can simulate this and make it as extreme as possible. You're worried about the language of innovation? Go and have Mandarin lessons. You're worried about creating a clear vision for your people? Go and learn how to paint. You're worried about taking risks? Go sky-diving or bungee-jumping.

By the time you're back at work facing your fears, it'll be child's play.

11. Just a little white lie

Finally, try lying a little bit. Let me rephrase that; exaggerate. You'll be surprised that a tiny bit of exaggeration can lead to a supremely enhanced feeling of creative stature.

The trick is to always have this in your mind: that you will at some point achieve your exaggeration, which means you are not actually lying, just getting your timelines a little out of order. As we really don't understand how time works (there were six or seven dimensions at last count), it's an understandable mistake.

Call it illusionary visioning, and then be sure to make the illusion a reality.

Now you've tried a few of those things, we hope you've started to feel innovation pulsing through your body. Now it's time to start doing something with it. Start simply. An anonymous member of the team recalls a story from his youth:

I admit I spent some time in nightclubs back in my reckless days. I would spy someone across the smoky dance floor and spend hours thinking of elaborate first lines that would make me seem like the most impressive dude of all time. Funnily enough this method met with little success. The last time I tried it I made up this story about being a professional musician in the midst of a world tour (I didn't really think about how ridiculous this seemed in a dodgy backstreet sweatbox in Stoke-on-Trent).

I was just about to approach the northern goddess I had identified and sweep her off her feet with my genius chat up lines when the competition turned up. This guy walked straight up to the girl I'd identified as my future spouse and said, 'Hi, my name is Dave.' Within one minute young Dave was doing more than talking. Since then I've always favoured keeping it as simple as possible. This may sound obvious, but you get better results and importantly you bring people along for the ride.

If your innovation juices are beginning to flow, start slowly (remember the brightly-coloured socks) and build up the bravery quotient.

As we explored in the last chapter, there are millions of role models out there and we asked you to use some of them to develop your innovation leadership beliefs. But you can also use these to help you flick on your innovation switch by thinking about traits and behaviours that help you be more innovative. To get people in the right place to innovate, we often ask them to think of others who really inspire them and why. We ask them to do this as a bit of homework, which works as great stimulus to get them engaged and thinking creatively before they even walk in the room.

Why don't you do this now? Think about someone who really inspires you – write out the story of why they inspire you and what their traits are. Now look through the list of traits or behaviours and think about how you could turn the volume up a little bit on some of them. You'll find some easier than others, but if you consciously start bringing some of those traits to life, you'll be surprised to see how innovative you will feel, not to mention quite proud of yourself.

Imagine if one of the behaviours you listed was *great at listening*, and one day you just listened more than you would do normally when people were talking directly to you. That's not difficult, but by that simple act you're taking steps towards adopting the traits of the most inspiring person you can imagine. Try ramping up a new one each week and see the results.

Let's reflect on the behaviours that you need to be a leader for innovation. Think about the variety of role models that people come up with and learn from: from parents to literary figures, from celebrities to military leaders, from work colleagues to politicians, and even animals. Think about the activities in this chapter and the behaviours you'll need to undertake them. Don't worry about getting anything wrong; those traits and behaviours will and can grow over time. If you are feeling brave run what you're doing past some of your closest team members and let them critique it with you (this could be a brave step in itself).

dangerous quest

Do you think anyone, including some of your closest team members, would put you on their list of role models? Take on this little challenge to get on as many lists as possible. While you are thinking about behaviours, think about your team, colleagues and the people around you. What qualities have they got that can help you?

Remember, just because you are striving to be a brilliant leader for innovation doesn't mean you have to do it on your own. Are you the ideas trailblazer, does everyone turn to you when they have got a problem and need a creative solution? Do they rely on you too much or do you *think* they rely on you too much?

dangerous quest

Create a problem which needs help from your people to solve, and then go on holiday. See how many new ideas arrive on your desk when you get back. You may be surprised, and may find that it isn't actually all down to you.

At the start of this chapter we asked you to write down all the things you were worried about doing this week and to imagine yourself stepping over a red line every time you achieved one. The next step is to actively approach and cross the red line out of choice, in your time and on your terms, taking as much control back as you can. We'll be exploring how to do this consciously over the next few chapters.

key learning points

- Take a deep breath and remember the red line of courage.
- Try adopting some little techniques or activities – from our list of 11 – that help you be more creative and innovative. Once you have tried them don't stop there. As a leader it is critical to your own development to keep experimenting and trying out new ones that keep pushing YOU.
- Be conscious of the behaviours you need to support you in being a leader and in being more creative and innovative.
- Think about your organisation, your own team, your colleagues – where is there opportunity to be more innovative no matter where you work?
- And finally, do something to find out how dependent your team are on you to be the creative or innovative person in the room (definitely before the next two chapters).

WORD CLOUD

chapter 4

unleashing the creative beast

One of the biggest misconceptions about innovation is that you should just let your people go and be innovative – on everything, everywhere, anytime. Why is that? It makes sense, doesn't it? Make innovation an everyday activity and surely it will flourish...Perhaps.

It might be controversial but when you want to unleash the creative beast in your team, you first need to give them a little bit of focus and structure. Then you need to keep them delivering. Above all, they need permission to be more innovative in the right areas and in the right way, as a clear and controlled demonstration of trust.

IF YOU CHASE TWO RABBITS, BOTH WILL ESCAPE

When planning for innovation and creativity it's important to set some context and answer the following question: Just how innovative do you want people to be, and in relation to which activities or projects?

dangerous quest

Write down all the things that you and your team are doing, and then think about how much innovation you need in each of them.

Many people talk about there being a scale of innovation; we mentioned it briefly in Chapter 1. At one end is revolution-driven innovation. Very few companies actually operate at this end. Perhaps the most famous of them all is Apple, a company we've already mentioned. At the other end is incremental innovation, innovations that move the organisation and industry on step by step. We consider each end of the scale to be equally valid.

Innovation Scale

Evolution ⟸⟹ Revolution

Incremental
Target ideas that
move the business
on step by step

Altering
New to your
organisation
ideas that reshape
your world

Breakthrough
New to world
'radical' ideas

Runners – These are the little problems and fixes that you do on a regular basis. In essence, they require targeted creativity in resolving these challenges. But they don't really create any new value, focusing as they do on retaining the original value that was already designed in. These are often referred to as improvement-led innovations.

So if you run a finance department, you don't want to be developing a new way of doing things every month; it would drive people up the wall. However, you might add in some simple colour or better classifications to help people fill the form in.

Altering – These are about developing innovations that push the product, service or change that next little step on. They focus the innovation effort on developing a new element or feature, rather than a radical solution.

For example, if you work in HR, you might be offering a new employee benefits package that's a little bit different, but still sits alongside all the other ones.

Breakthrough – These are about developing radical solutions and innovations. They look to create the next generation, the new platform, the big leap forward. They ask the big questions and look for the bigger solutions.

For example, if you were working in procurement, this might involve developing a new order management system that is a completely different way for anybody ordering anything in the business, completely replacing the old system.

These three classifications are nothing new (we've seen them broken down into five different levels, with innovation as a research activity which may not initially lead to anything new, and a 'no innovation' level). But what these categories do is help you as a leader to clearly signal what type of innovation is desired, plan for an appropriate set of activities to be undertaken to develop and deliver the desired level of innovation, i.e., the process for delivering an incremental innovation does not have to be as comprehensive as the one for a stranger, as well as maintain the focus in your team. Importantly, they also help you to spot when the level of innovation changes, so you can manage expectations accordingly. This helps you keep a dialogue open with the team and stops you 'jumping in', an act that many teams associate with the removal of permission.

THE SAUSAGE MACHINE

Dangerous thinking comes when you layer the *how* on top of your ambitions.

The challenge for many departments and teams is that they are often awash with ideas. OK, many of them might be ill-conceived, unfocused and slightly random. But the plain fact is that there usually is an 'ideas vault' archived in some dusty corner of a server that contains a host of ideas that never made it. They were a little different, perhaps a little quirky; maybe even a little wayward in thinking.

Imagine your team makes sausages. It has a fantastic operation for manufacturing them. It has customers who love them. Its mental model is a string of sausages: pork meat in the middle, skin on the outside.

Now you come along with an idea, just a little idea. It's basically a vegetarian hamburger: vegetables, carefully blended into a pattie, with fresh wholemeal bread baps to go with it. New customers are going to love it. You start working on it. What happens next?

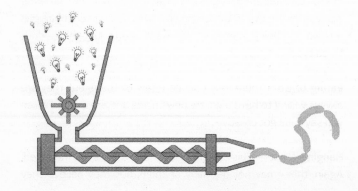

The answer is that in many teams, it still ends up as a sausage. And yes, customers like it, but they almost certainly don't love it as much as they would have liked the original idea.

What happened? Why did it end that way?

The story above is a true one – and we have seen it in many teams. In this case it was a communications team in a big organisation we know. They were always coming up with great ideas for communicating stuff to employees, like graffiti on the pavement outside the front door to tell staff about some new awards, or a billboard on the bike shed. But everything ended up as a newsletter. So why is that? It's because newsletters are their sausages.

Now this isn't about playing to one's strengths, which is important. It's the fact that their breakthrough innovations never made it and consequently they missed out on a major change in their marketplace. Think Kodak films and digital photos. Get the picture?

How do you get over this? The answer lies in a simple truth. The more innovative you want the product to be, the more innovative the approach to developing that new innovation has to be – the how.

WHO'S IN YOUR TEAM?

Stand back and think about the people in your team. There are many different types of personality when it comes to being in a team and being innovative. We want you to just think about three types:

Raring to Go – There may only be a few of them, but they are always willing to have a go, try new things and are excited when you say 'let's get creative'.

Hanging Back – This second group are a little bit reserved. Again, there may not be many of them, but they believe they could be creative or innovative if they tried. Some people see them as difficult, but that's not necessarily true. They could have confidence problems or be stuck in a rut. Either way, they take a lot of work and encouragement.

Me Too – This is the rest of the team, the majority of the group. As their name suggests they are reactive and are often swayed by a situation or the people they're working with.

Now you have a handle on who is in your team, there are a number of things you can do with each of these groups to get the innovation wave going.

Establish your first followers, with the Raring to Go gang

We firmly believe that ideas and innovation are really hard to pursue on your own. It is much easier in a group or at least with a friend or colleague who has energy and enthusiasm. You need others with whom to share your thoughts and to help you get started and to give you the confidence to continue.

Have you ever had an idea and been to afraid to share it just in case everyone thinks you are mad or that the idea is rubbish? If you have then you definitely need to follow the next step or you will never make a difference. Being a great innovation leader means you have to be brave and demonstrate your bravery to your colleagues.

Share those ideas, win over people

In Chapter 2 we asked you to watch a video on YouTube. Did you do it? If not, go back and watch it. It's actually quite important because it demonstrated quite perfectly the concept of the First Follower. By the way, we have no intention of taking any credit for this theory. We just really like it and if you apply it to the subject of innovation, it can be extremely helpful.

With respect to the Raring to Go people, we just want you to think about finding and recruiting your first follower. Start small, perhaps a chat over a coffee to sound out your intentions with a close colleague or a friend. Of course, if you want to be more stretching, you can push ahead and recruit a few more of the Raring to Go gang.

With this small band of followers, we want you to become a real role model to help them focus and hone their innovation so they become a group of quite capable people. As they are always enthusiastic, tap into that energy and get them to help you encourage others in your team, especially those who sit in the Me Too group. BUT choose your first follower carefully as it could be seen as favouritism. Once you've done this, you will never have to stand up as the one lone nut.

Flexing the how for the Hanging Back people

As we have said before, you can't flick a switch and expect everybody to be innovative straight away, especially this group. Change just isn't that simple. It's like saying to a toddler: 'You're 14 months old now. Get up and walk!' and expecting them to walk perfectly there and then.

It's important to be realistic about what people in your team can do and achieve.

Therefore with this group it's about considering all the levers you can pull and changing one dimension slightly to prompt them to see that they can be more innovative by getting them to be more creative about how they go about their tasks.

Possible levers include:

- Operating mindset – run the project like a new company whether inside or temporarily outside the business.
- Location – move from area to area, from inside to outside the office.

- Environment – a very important lever. This can include everything from the desks, through to a purpose-built environment or a temporary space.
- Duration – go from time-boxed jobs (fixed period of time) to time-slotted work (fixed days, e.g. Tuesdays).
- Who's involved, when, how much? – consider the size of the team and its make-up: part time/full time, core versus extended, the blend of expertise, the different roles.
- Path/steps/phases – look at the overall process, the degree of flexibility, the phasing (see next section).
- Methodology or approach – the toolkit, the degree of co-design, use of open innovation etc.
- Budget versus investment – believe it or not, this can be a lever.
- Additional resources – including customers, naive experts, suppliers, unusual skills or the unusual suspects.
- Glory and rewards – these don't have to be monetary; in fact the best ones aren't. They can be used to celebrate 'learned failure' too.

The key is to observe what's happening when and by whom, and then change just one dimension to make it just a little bit more innovative.

For example, when people are undertaking projects, where do they work? We guarantee that it is mainly at a desk or in a meeting room. What if they went to where the customer is and did the project there?

Let's look at desks. How is your area laid out? Is everybody sitting in their own little desk space, and are there partitions? What if they sat around one big Viking-style desk, with their own space but working together as a team?

What about the environment (really important) around them? Do they bring their work to life for others to see and comment on, with pictures or illustrations or even mock-ups on their walls and desks around them?

Remember, this is about getting the wave going. The benefit is that it enables these people to see that they can do a little thing to help them feel a little more innovative. And they will become more open to the next set of ideas too.

HARNESS INNOVATION - IN THE DAY-TO-DAY LIFE OF THE TEAM

Do any of these statements apply to your team members?

- They work hard, but when it comes to being innovative they are still waiting for instruction.
- Individually they are different, but they don't always play to their strengths.
- Sometimes, they don't always capitalise on their roles and influence with stakeholders.
- They easily fall back on tried and trusted ways, even though they know it's not stretching them to be innovative.

The challenge with any team is to establish the right habits, keep the focus and help people to stay in their Stretch zones (see Chapter 5). If you dissect your team's working life you can identify where and when to embed a few simple things that help to break up the sausage machine and keep innovation flowing:

1. **Stand-ups** – daily 10 minute team briefing and team connection time.

2. **Weekly wash-ups** – a way of bringing each week to a close and celebrating little successes.

3. **Creative coaching checkpoints** – reviews designed to give people coaching support.

4. **Sharing sessions** – to promote the sharing of learning and experiences between team members.

5. **Continual communication** – thinking of different ways to get around one-way methods.

6. **Creative surgeries** – to promote the use and application of creativity.

7. **Going on safari** – to get people to experience other worlds, and other ways of doing things.

We've expanded on each of these below. They all have varying degrees of difficulty, so feel free to start with those that will make the most difference. And if you are doing some of them already, check that you have the emphasis right.

1. Stand-ups

So simple they are often overlooked in an office environment, stand-ups are very effective. Devised originally in manufacturing as a method for cell teams (self-directed teams that own and operate their area in production almost as a mini-business) to come together and prepare for the shift ahead, this simple approach is ideal for innovation teams. The basic concept of stand-ups is to promote team unity, face to face communication and understanding. They also give you a chance to provide 30 seconds of coaching to each member, if it's needed.

In an office environment, they work like this. Every morning the team gathers around a planning board for 10 minutes, and in turn each person:

- says how they are and if anything is holding them back from being in the right zone;
- reviews how they got on the day before and where they got to;
- outlines their plan for the day;
- identifies any support needs.

It's straightforward, simple and effective and you can also incorporate other things. For example, Ritz Carlton incorporate a key theme for the day or week into each of their daily stand-ups. But whatever you do, keep it short and sweet. If it turns into a big meeting, it's not working. AND don't be afraid to take issues out of the session to be dealt with separately.

2. Weekly wash-ups

These are massively important. They are about bringing the week to a close and making sure everything is reflected on. Appropriate steps can be taken for the coming week, preventing anything from sliding. This is probably the most controlled thing you can do. It stops people from just drifting off for the weekend, and it's your chance to give people praise for their achievements during the week.

Weekly wash-ups don't have to be long. If you've been doing daily stand-ups, then it will be a breeze. If not, then it will take a bit more effort, but it will pay off. We have run multimillion budget programmes with this approach, but they work equally well on small projects.

If you want to get really structured, look at the team's individual weekly project plans and personal development reviews. This makes everything very, very transparent.

You will have to fight hard for this time, so make sure everybody has it in their diary well in advance. It's the one time people always want to bite into. Whatever happens, you can always get people to phone or video call in (think James Bond with plasma TVs on the wall for each team member) or provide an update via a colleague.

3. Reviews or, preferably, creative coaching checkpoints

Are your reviews:

- boring?
- one-sided: one person speaks while the others listen?
- rigidly structured?
- skating over the issues?
- talking shop with no passion or commitment?
- worse, completely paper-based?

It's much better to have a variety of reviews to match different moments in the journey, offering the chance to reflect on where the innovation project has got to, providing advice and support, understanding the challenges going forward and then commissioning the next step.

These can be fun, engaging, short or long, interactive...and deadly creative, especially in the *how*. Here are a few examples:

Watering Holes

SRI in the US are famed for an approach called Watering Holes. Broadly, these are designed to help people who are trying to frame their ideas into propositions. They are open, held at a regular time each week and use a set structure to help them flow. When people want to pause and reflect on their project, they go along to a Watering Hole. They pitch their proposition in a specific way and get feedback from everybody around them. You can make progress without doing this, it's an informal check point, but the people doing it get help, support and coaching.

Interactive stage reviews

When Motor Coach Industries were developing their new set of buses, they put in place some simple but interactive stage reviews in their studio facility based around a mock-up of the bus. Executives and senior management were asked to help them review progress. During the review of the mock-up, they would put coloured stickers (red – no, amber – warning, green – yes) marked with their initials, on a huge key deliverables chart on the wall. This kept it all visual and very transparent. It also helped them understand who they needed to talk to during the next stages to resolve issues before they happened.

Child's play

Unilever Brazil ran a project review for a new product aimed at families. They chose to run the review in a children's soft play centre. This kept young families in the minds of the people there. It also kept the review tied to the very market for which they were developing the product.

Role-play

We once ran a review as a play. We set up a small set to mimic a customer environment, in this case a producing studio. We had some actors role-play how the proposition would work. We also brought in some friendly customers to provide some advice and support to the team (one of the actors was then hired by a customer to help on an internal programme they were running).

Whatever you do, taking this simple approach to how you structure things can really help plan the slow release of the creative potential of your team.

4. Sharing sessions

Sharing sessions build on the above, ensuring learning is transferred between projects. They are not about reviews; they are about creating self-awareness and a self-development culture in the team, making sure that learning is constantly extracted and shared and helping to spread and reinforce innovation. Again, these sessions are best kept short, sweet and at high intensity – almost workout style.

We would also suggest giving them themes: Customers Count, Stakeholders are Human Too, Prototyping Pitfalls, Design Disasters, Impactful Project Launches, for example. And try putting them on video with a simple camcorder or mobile phone, and uploading them to an intranet portal for easy access. You can direct new joiners to them to aid their learning, or use them as a reference for the team.

5. Continual communication

Email, intranet pages, voicemail. Are any of these suitable for communication? How many people these days actually read their email and register what is written? Just because you have sent it, doesn't mean they have read it or understood it. Successful innovation leadership often sees communication as more engagement orientated, and not just a one-off activity.

There are no hard and fast rules here. Some of the tools above will help you to boost communication, and continual communication with your team is a necessary fact of life. In the same way that product launches have communication plans, preparing to unleash the beast means having a communication plan in place too, one that will help you think through what you signal, to whom, when and what the outcomes will be.

However, communication must be two-way; what communication do you want to receive from your team, and when?

It's worth taking the time to think about this; after all, miscommunication is the root of all evil.

6. Creative surgeries

Creative surgeries build on some of the principles of Watering Holes. They can be used with your team to help focus their creativity as well as receive input in an open and constructive way. The basic approach involves regular 60–90 minute sessions where a member of the team presents a challenge they are working on, together with where they are and the outcomes they want from the session. This enables them to get both a creative reflection and ideas from their colleagues. The product of these sessions is lots of thoughts, ideas and reframing for the team member to think about and take forward. The bi-product is also sharing between team members and the passing of ideas and approaches from one to another.

A real imperative for these sessions is maintaining appropriate building behaviours, rather than the close-down equivalent. This of course creates a great opportunity for you to role model these behaviours too. However, as with most things, the key is getting your team to own and drive them, even when you are not there.

7. Going on safari

We are big fans of expeditions to new worlds, experiencing new things that can really help you to break the mould in your organisation. In other words, going on an innovation safari.

There are many benefits: raising confidence, refreshing your personal stimulus bank, spotting other ideas to enrich your own, even questioning or reframing the challenge you are actually trying to solve. The funny thing is, many companies don't do it, or when they do, it's half-hearted.

Safaris are not a jolly. They are certainly not slapdash. To be effective they need to be carefully researched and designed to match the challenge you are facing, set up correctly with the team (*this is where we are going, why and how we need to go about it*), then undertaken in the right spirit. Finally, the debrief, or landing, should be done very thoroughly on the same day the safari is held. The feeling you want from people is 'Wow, I'm knackered. This was hard work but very illuminating.'

In the 1970s and 1980s the Japanese were masters of the innovation safari. They set up lots of exchange visits with other companies, even competitors, who let them in with open arms. However, they only used this tool to learn and catch up; they didn't use it to push themselves forward.

Rather than focus on the way to do it, let's have a look at the pitfalls. Avoid these and any safari you do – big or small – will work great:

Safari Pitfalls
Not focused enough
You can go out and get any experience, but this only serves to release any mental block you might have. To be effective you really need to do your homework. What challenge are you facing? In industries other than your own, who can you learn from and what can you learn? How can you approach them? Is there anything you can do to give them fresh insight too?

Ideas mode, not observation mode
We are big fans of spotting others' ideas and learning from them. However, we are not fans of spotting others' ideas and embedding them lock, stock and barrel into what we do; they don't always fit. An airline infrastructure company we know saw in other organisations the power of mission control rooms, where all the programmes across the business are visible and tracked. They took this idea as they saw it and embedded it in their organisation. Consequently, it became a room full of charts that nobody looked at and which were only updated when one person had the time. It was dropped six months later. 'We tried

that,' they said, 'and it didn't work'. What they didn't do was stand back and consider their own issues and how the idea could be developed to address problems in their environment. Their issue was visibility rather than management control, and visibility of the programme could be tracked differently, for example, with a traffic light system on a mission control style web portal.

Making it too long

People run out of energy and get overloaded. It's a fine art, but its best to address a few things quickly and well, rather than creating one long crusade.

Not the right people in the safari team

Think about it. Going on safari with a like-minded group will only serve to reinforce their like-mindedness. You need fresh perspectives too, especially when trying to encourage different ideas.

Drifting away at the end

This is in two parts: never landing at all or landing too long after the safari, which is just as bad. Too long can be as little as a couple of hours, let alone days. When you are back at base, other things creep in and memory fades. Landing needs to be planned into the visit so it's part of the activity. Don't let anybody go until it's done.

SETTING A CLEAR PATH FOR YOUR TEAM'S INNOVATION DEVELOPMENT

In the spirit of innovation, setting a clear path has two parts. The first is the path for your team, the second is the path they take when developing a new innovation.

We find most teams have devised a raison d'être for who they are and what they do in their department or company. In most cases this is linked to the strategy of the business, and they have a plan for the type of work and projects they'll take on. They may even have an outline of how they are going to deliver them too – the second part of the path. However, what we don't find is an outline of where they are now and the development steps they need to take to get there. Is it a sign of weakness? We don't think so.

Firstly, it is important to acknowledge their starting place and how you enable them to develop and try out new-found behaviours and skills on their projects. But it also enables you to be realistic about how much support or time they are going to need – remember the switch.

As you start to build confidence in them you can focus on embedding the day-in-day-out disciplines, tools and techniques that boost innovation across the team, before finally getting them onto the path of being an amazing innovation outfit that everybody either wants to be in or wants to own.

WHEN IT BECOMES A WASTE OF TIME

Somebody once said you are only as good as the last thing you delivered. So just talking about or polishing your ideas amounts to nothing in the end. The challenge as a leader of innovation is treading that fine line between building creativity and innovation in your team, and knowing when you need to say 'Stop! We need to move on and deliver.'

Let's be honest, you are always going to get a few people who say they have tried to be more innovative but it didn't quite work. Well, as we have shown you, you can change these people slowly but surely, but this isn't about them. This is about being mindful of the people who love the feeling of freedom that creativity and innovation brings but act as though they don't need to think about delivery. These people often get stuck in the process, in a mindset of constant iteration, and not trusting their own judgement to move on. They are the first to offer help to others who want to get ideas into a process, often to the detriment of their own projects.

Innovation is about developing something that has been refined into a finished article that customers and service users want and love. But it isn't about going back over the same ground hoping to find some additional value-adding insight, when that won't actually make the proposition more appealing. It isn't just about ideas; it's about delivering the right amount of new value to a customer.

One behaviour you need as a leader is to 'learn fast, kill quick'. The principle is to spot the projects that won't deliver what's needed and kill them quickly. Many people will feel this is a failure, but actually it's a success. If you can learn from the project and then stop it fast, you will actually enable your innovation resources to get behind the ones that are really going to deliver. This stops projects becoming drawn-out affairs that never implement. As a leader, there is skill in ensuring the project is stopped quickly and in an appropriate way. At first people might not like it, but eventually they will thank you for it; as long as it's done in a spirit of innovation.

Finally, it's crucial to get some quick wins when you start to get the innovation wave going. It keeps the wolf from the door and creates some energy in the team and belief that the new way works.

key learning points

- Think about how innovative you want your team to be – and what focus you need to give them to help make sure they're still productive.
- Think about your team. Who could be a first follower and who would benefit from small changes to help them be more innovative?
- Build in some simple daily structures that enable team and individual innovation to flourish, even when you are not there.
- You still have a job to do and you need to make sure you deliver, so you need to develop a keen foresight to say 'we've learned enough from this one but...'
- Just get going. Don't worry about strategies yet. The art of an innovation leader is to build consciously from within.

WORD CLOUD

chapter 5
lighting the creative fires

o hopefully you've primed yourself to be in your personal innovation zone and set up the right structures for your team's creativity to blossom. We also hope you've spotted some specific innovation leadership behaviours, and possibly one or two capabilities. That's great; keep going.

But now it's time to start seeking out and lighting creative fires...That may sound dangerous, fire can burn after all, and if you haven't got the right foundations in place it certainly can be. However, like all the chapters in this book, it's up to you how dangerous you want to be.

So how do we measure the level of danger you want to go for? In Chapter 3 we talked about consciously crossing the red line. Well there's a simple exercise to work out where you are on the innovation and danger spectrum and where that line is for your team.

GETTING INTO THE ZONE

Practise this exercise on your own first and then do it with your team. Here's how it works. Before your team arrive, get three pieces of A4 paper (make them coloured if you're feeling really daring), a thick felt pen and a roll of masking tape. Find a clear bit of floor space and mark out two parallel lines on the floor with the masking tape. Make them about 2 metres long and about 2 metres apart. Then write in big letters, 'Comfort Zone' on the first piece of paper, 'Stretch Zone' on the second and 'Panic Zone' on the third. Keep these to one side.

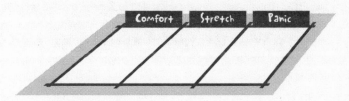

That's the preparation bit done. Now, get your team to come into the room and ask them all to stand together behind one of the lines of masking tape (i.e. not in between the two lines).

The Comfort Zone

Show them your homemade Comfort Zone sign, and ask if anyone has heard of it. It's a common phrase so most people will probably have. Ask them what it feels like when they are in their Comfort Zone. Encourage people to shout out their answers. You'll get loads of suggestions: calm, relaxed, chilled, comfortable, soothing, in control. Some may well use language like boring, dull, unchallenging. If they don't get to this try prompting them: 'Is it an exciting place to be?' When they have all had their say, summarise their key words and highlight that it can be nice and relaxed but a bit boring too. Finish by stating that from now on anywhere behind this line is the Comfort Zone and place your sign on the floor to mark it.

The Panic Zone

Then, ask them all to go and stand behind the other line (i.e. again, not in between the two lines of masking tape) and ask them to guess what they think the exact opposite zone of the Comfort Zone is. People will guess – the danger zone, the discomfort zone, the horrible zone. Tell them it's the Panic Zone and ask them what it feels like to be there. As before, listen to their suggestions and summarise. If they are struggling, tell a story of when you have been in your Panic Zone. Describe what was happening and how you were feeling. You know the times: when the phone is ringing, your boss is waiting for that report, you've got a customer waiting, you're up against a seemingly impossible deadline...

The Stretch Zone

Next, ask the group to stand in between the two lines and

explain that this area is called the Stretch Zone. Ask them what they think this zone feels like and what happens when they are there. They will most probably tell you that it feels challenging, exciting, nerve-jangling, learning, stretching, pushing. Summarise their thoughts about the Stretch Zone, and add this: it's the place to learn, feel nervously excited and challenged, and where you can really grow as a person. Importantly for you as a leader for innovation, it is the place where you will generate new ideas and be brave.

Make it personal

Now, ask them to go and stand in the zone they feel they are in right now. Make a mental note of their positions – you may be surprised at what you see. Explain that you are going to read out a number of 'scientifically' created scenarios and you would like them to stand in the zone that they would go to if this scenario was about to happen to them. Here are a few example scenarios that we know work really well, but feel free to add in your own (and pick selectively from this list). You will notice that they start with some distance from the workplace and get closer.

Try creating some scenarios which are really relevant to your specific workplace so the exercise lands back in your world:

- Watch two football (soccer) matches back to back at home on TV.
- Run around this room naked.
- Make dinner for everybody in this room.
- Your mother-in-law is coming to stay today.
- Go to your first foreign language lesson.
- Go bungee jumping right now.
- Spend Sunday with your family.
- Go to London to see the sights.
- Run a marathon tomorrow.
- Drive to work.

- Sing your favourite song in front of everyone right now.
- Juggle four balls.
- Order lobster in a restaurant.
- Go on holiday to Australia.
- Play a game of Monopoly.
- Read *The Lord of the Rings*.
- Go shopping for new clothes.
- Tell a joke to everyone in the room.
- In two hours you have to do a one hour presentation to the main board of directors.
- Do an interview with national TV about the organisation and your role in helping it be successful.
- Get to work and discover that all your colleagues have resigned.
- Challenge a colleague about their unacceptable behaviour at work.
- Speak directly to your customers to ask how your organisation can be improved.
- Share ideas for making things better for each other and for your customers.

Allow people a short amount of time after each scenario you describe to think about how they would react, and then ask them to move to the relevant zone. They can pick their spot within the zone to add a little more colour to their choice: if they chose to stand in the Stretch Zone are they closer to the Comfort Zone or the Panic Zone?

Ask a few of the team why they are standing where they are. Listen to their stories and again make a mental note of where people have put themselves but remember that this is not an exact science. After each scenario you will really start to see a picture emerging of the differences in your team. You will see those who like to take risks, you will see who's very experienced, you will see who will need more support, and so on.

After you have shared a scenario like cooking for everyone in the room, dig into why people are standing where they are. If they are in the Panic Zone is it because they can't cook, they don't like cooking or is it the people who are here, or is it the sheer number of people? You'll find a variety of answers. Asking the same question of someone in the Comfort Zone may highlight the experience they have of catering for large numbers, but further questioning might reveal their fears the first time they had to cook for a large number of people. There will be journeys in the room from which everyone can learn.

The last scenario relates directly to your creative challenges ahead, so it will give you a great sense of who could be your Creative Champions (we'll talk a bit more about this later) and who your key allies will be in getting the innovation ball rolling in your organisation or department.

Finally, ask this question: Where should our collective ambition for innovation and change be? Of course, the answer should, and will be, in the Stretch Zone.

Bringing it together

When you've finished going through your scenarios, summarise by pulling out a few key points:

- We all stood in different places for every scenario, so all of us reacted differently in different situations. Therefore, we need to be aware of how we can support each other and use the strengths within the team to help us work together in the best possible way.
- We also need to think about which zone our other colleagues will be in and, of course, which zone our customers will be in, and work out what impact our decisions will have on them and how they will be feeling in their different scenarios.
- The more times we visit the Stretch Zone the bigger our Comfort Zone will get – practice and experience is key.

- The Stretch Zone is an exciting place to be but it can take some effort and bravery to get there.
- If we want to improve, and be creative and innovative together as a team, we are going to have to step into our Stretch Zone every day and support each other when we are there.

an example of this in action

We once ran the zones exercise with a large group of hotel managers in Holland, and when we shared the second scenario – run around this room naked – one chap stood in the Comfort Zone whilst the rest of the group were understandably all in the Panic Zone (which is the norm by the way). Before we could ask him why, and commend him on his bravery, he had stripped off every inch of clothing and was sprinting around the room throwing in the occasional cartwheel. This was obviously quite a shocking sight for the rest of the audience but it did, however, illustrate quite wonderfully how different we all are. An extreme scenario for many people is maybe not so extreme to others. It was a good job they were all seasoned hotel professionals and had seen more than one naked guest turn up at their reception desks and streak along their corridors.

dangerous quest

A nice addition to this exercise is to compare your expectations of the team, from your observations of them working together normally, with how they actually react as you run the session. How good is your judgement of your team?

So, you understand the desire, potential and capability of your team, and they do too. You have introduced some simple language around creativity (Which zone are you in today? Was that a Stretch Zone idea? and so on) that you can start using regularly until it becomes part of your daily team routines. You have engaged the team in a way that may well be very different for them, signalling that a change is coming. And you and the team have agreed a collective and simple ambition for innovation and change in a non-threatening way.

Now it's time to start giving people permission to be creative.

GIVING PERMISSION

This may sound like an unnecessary step in the process but it is one of the most essential. If you don't give your team the permission to express themselves with new ideas, you will end up with a mixture of three outcomes:

1. No one will give you any ideas.

2. Any ideas you do get will be 'Comfort Zone' ideas.

3. One or two influential people will flourish, possibly to the detriment of everyone else.

All in all not a great result. Permission can be given in many ways but you can't just tell everyone that they now have permission to be innovative. The first step, as we've alluded to in earlier chapters, is to show how innovative you would like people to be and in what forum you would like them to express their creativity, through leading by example.

If you are looking for quick, little ideas for improvement, think of a few yourself to get the ball rolling. Make sure that they are pitched at the right level so people can gauge what you are looking for. Suggest a few whacky ideas so that your people understand it's okay to be a bit radical. Even try throwing in the odd idea that will stimulate debate or get shot down in flames. It all helps people to know exactly what is allowed.

dangerous quest

Whatever your role in the organisation, you probably have someone to answer to in the hierarchy: your immediate boss, shareholders or, in the case of the public sector, the public themselves. Be mindful of how much permission you have to do things your way and for how long. Work out the benefits to the organisation, your staff and your customers, and illustrate what changes might be seen. It will help your 'bosses' to be supportive and avoid any surprises.

When asking your team to be creative, remind them that all their ideas should be in the Stretch Zone without being too stretching. Of course there need to be limits, so levels of permission should have boundaries. However, it is not too difficult to deduce where the creative boundary should be in your organisation. That's right, the top of the Stretch Zone.

Before we go any further, the challenge with leading for innovation and lighting fires in your team is to keep things simple and practical. We have deliberately chosen to stay with an approach where ideas are driven by people rather than by strategic market planning processes.

The golden rule when asking your people for ideas is to acknowledge their contribution. In general, people will share their ideas once. If nothing happens, they may share their ideas a second time. If nothing happens this time, they will give up. That's when disengagement starts in the organisation (a topic for another book).

Every successful organisation has at some point attempted to harness the power of their employees' creativity by asking them for their ideas, with widely varying results.

The first question to ask is why you are doing it. Is it:

1. to get great ideas that will improve your business for you and your customers?

2. to engage your workforce in making the organisation better?

Hopefully you've answered the question by saying a combination of both 1 and 2. That's all well and good, but it presents an exciting and potentially complex challenge.

case example

One of our favourite clients over the last few years was a large service provider and retailer with call centres across the UK and the all over the world.

Our clients were quite sure that the best people to help them improve their business, operationally and in terms of pure customer service, were their staff and, through them, their customers. Thousands of staff and millions of customers having tens of millions of conversations every year – what an opportunity to capture and use insight, trends, issues in the making, and simple customer feedback. This was too big an opportunity to miss.

This was the trigger for action: the CEO was on one of his usual unscheduled Friday afternoon visits to his call centres and as he wandered around he overheard a young adviser having what seemed to be a particularly tricky conversation with a customer. The CEO listened carefully and waited until the adviser had finished getting a severe telling off by his irate customer.

'What was that all about?' the CEO inquired. The young adviser went on to explain that the female customer was phoning to complain about being referred to as either Mr or Sir in all written correspondence. The CEO was obviously concerned, but his biggest cause of surprise was the strength and passion with which the customer had complained. He had even heard her raised tones creeping through the adviser's headphones.

Why was she so angry? Yes, it was sloppy, but surely just a small mistake that they could rectify immediately. He continued to quiz the adviser. Apparently the customer was particularly annoyed because this was the fifth time she'd phoned up to report the issue. The fifth time! The adviser went on to explain that in the six months he had been working there he had often received complaints about this issue, perhaps up to four or five times a week.

The CEO's mood changed from one of frustration to anger. 'So, what do you do when you get these complaints then?' he asked the bemused adviser. 'I used to fill in the complaints/ideas form and submit it, but I sent it so many times I figured head office must have got the message by now and someone must be working on it. I told my boss a few times too but she just told me to fill in the form. I suppose I thought four or five customers out of millions isn't too bad – mistakes are bound to happen.'

On investigation it turned out that over a million female customers were being referred to as Mr and Sir, so those fours and fives were adding up as no one was putting two and two together.

How could that happen, we hear you cry. Surely someone would have noticed.

Well, it's the age old problem of not closing the loop. If you ask for feedback you will get it, if you ask for ideas you will get them; so you have to be prepared for the flood that will undoubtedly come. Preparation is the key and that's where we helped when we got involved.

The company's attempts to harness the creative power of their people had gone a bit awry over the years. Their initial, admirable intention was that all staff, regardless of role or grade, could share their ideas, thoughts and customer feedback via an online tool which then fed back to a central team (in fact, one person in an office) who would distribute the information. Unfortunately, the system proved to be extremely successful at attracting feedback from day one, which meant the 'team' was overwhelmed from the outset. This led to much frustration at both ends of the chain. No responses came back to participants and there was barely a scratching of the surface of the information being received.

An executive decision was then made to use the online tool solely for big money making/saving ideas. This message never really filtered down to the front line, which meant that advisers and staff from across the organisation continued to use it as their only method of sharing customer feedback. At the other end of the chain, the majority of the feedback was ignored as it didn't meet the money generating/saving criteria. The situation only came to light after it had hacked off over a million customers.

Keeping ideas alive

Success in this case came when they worked on making sure the back end of the process – the people receiving and working on the ideas and issues – was as strong as the front end – the people submitting their ideas and feedback. The trick was to develop a process where all the people involved were working together to keep it alive, and benefit customers and the organisation. This involved managers coaching their staff around ideas and how to solve issues first time, and people coming together to look through the issues identified and develop ideas together to resolve them.

Secondly, many ideas seemed ill-conceived. This is often true because suggestions can be just an expression of the problem, or something that's been in a person's mind for some time. It's easy to be dismissive of suggestions; they are just thoughts after all.

However, if you look at them carefully, suggestions can be gold dust, because they are stimuli and can be re-engineered backwards to get to the problem. But they are not yet an idea, and that's the additional challenge for a leader because at this stage they are so easy to dismiss as valueless. As a leader, how can you know if you don't allow sufficient time for suggestions to be further developed? Consider these three levels of suggestion:

A creative thought
Something that's directional, gives you an angle on the problem, or just a wish, for example, brighten up reception.

An idea
A little better articulated, an idea is more descriptive of the possible answer and you can do something with it, for example, put flowers in reception every day.

A predefined solution
Something that contains a hidden technology or a specific answer that narrows it, and makes it hard to take or build into a deeper idea, for example, 12 daffodils in a blue vase on the right-hand shelf behind the reception desk.

If you are going to invite people to share their ideas and creativity you must have a process. We know the word process sounds counterproductive when applied to creativity and innovation but it's actually one of the essential ingredients. Look at the most ingenious artists and inventors – all of them have a process for being creative. They need a process which allows their brain to relax into creating something new and exciting, often out of nothing.

It doesn't matter whether you are running a workshop with 10 people or asking 20,000 people for their ideas; if you have a process coupled with the right creative behaviours, you can achieve anything.

dangerous quest

To start building your people-driven ideas process, there are some simple questions to ask yourself:

1. How many people could possibly give their ideas?

2. What do you want ideas about?

3. Do you want people to do some investigation into individual issues?

4. How are they going to submit their ideas?

5. How would you like them to structure their ideas?

6. Do they know the difference between a thought and an idea?

7. Do you want people to work on their own or in groups?

8. Who is going to receive these ideas?

9. How are you going to acknowledge people for their contribution?

10. What are you going to do with the ideas?

11. How can you turn these ideas into reality?

12. How can you keep the ideas momentum going?

So why ask all these questions? Let's dig a little bit deeper and see why they're important.

1. How many people could possibly give their ideas?

Imagine if you have 1,000 staff and they each submit three ideas each on average. That's a minimum of 3,000 ideas. Can you cope with that? Have you got a team in place to deal with those volumes? Our advice is start with your immediate team and see how you go.

2. What do you want ideas about?

Do you want general ideas or is there a specific issue or challenge? The more specific you are, the more focused the ideas.

3. Do you want people to do some investigation into individual issues?

You can ask your team to do some research first; it will start them thinking. They can look at competitors or ask customers, friends and family for their thoughts.

4. How are they going to submit their ideas?

Word of mouth, paper, online, a big board in the office...?

5. How would you like them to structure their ideas?

Do you want the headline or the detail as well? How will it work, who will it affect, what will it cost, what is the impact, what else would we need to make it work?

6. Do they know the difference between a thought and an idea?

You can generate ideas from thoughts but thoughts aren't much use to you unless you want to come up with all the ideas yourself. Give everyone an example to help them out. *The food in the canteen needs improving* is a thought; *ask the head chef from the Chinese restaurant next door for some advice on improving our canteen menu* is an idea.

7. Do you want people to work on their own or in groups?

The format of your approach is paramount to its success – a workshop, a team meeting, on the job or as part of a big overarching process?

8. Who is going to receive these ideas?

Do you want the people who generate the ideas to keep ownership of them or are you putting a team in place to do it?

9. How are you going to acknowledge people for their contribution?

A simple thank you and an update on progress is usually enough.

10. What are you going to do with the ideas?

Are you going to build them into something bigger by bringing them together?

11. How can you turn these ideas into reality?

What does the short-, medium- and long-term plan look like?

12. How can you keep the ideas momentum going?

What other little things can you do to maintain the excitement?

These are simple questions to ask yourself before you go any further. You don't need to have all the answers, but keep them in mind as you go through your innovation journey. Again, start close to home with you and your team before you go out to the wider business.

IDEAS WORKSHOPS

We think the easiest and most effective way of getting the creative fires blazing in your organisation is to run some simple idea-generation workshops. Start with your immediate team, a cross-section of people from across your business, or a mix of the two.

An ideas workshop, however, isn't as simple as sitting in a room having a brainstorming session. It takes three different key ingredients, what we call the 3Ss:

- Stimulus
- Structure
- Speed (not a word often associated with the creative process)

Here's an example of an ideas workshop flow that you can use to bring the 3Ss to life for you and your team. This session can take up to a day to run, but if time is tight you can achieve a lot in as little as three hours. To make it as real as possible let's use an example – imagine you are the customer service initiatives team in the head office of a medium-sized retail business that is reasonably new to the market.

The brief

After commissioning some initial research into the demographics of your customers, you have identified that more than 25 per cent are over 55 years old and the indications are that this is growing. In terms of the customer service you provide, you do nothing specific for this age group. What can you do for this group to earn their continued loyalty and willingness to recommend you to their friends and family?

Preparation (assuming about 15 attendees)

Make sure you have a room big enough for everyone to move about freely. We recommend having a horseshoe of chairs at the front of the room around a flip chart, with a number of tables at the back to allow people to work in groups of four or five. If you want people to be creative you don't want them to feel like they are coming to a board meeting. They need space in which to be creative, and by building two distinct areas in the room you can create changes in energy throughout the session.

We ran a creative ideas session with frontline staff of a healthcare provider. The venue was a seminar room in a hospital. We redesigned the room to allow the people attending to be creative, sticking up loads of pictures relating to their challenge (patients, customers, different equipment etc.) and coloured paper covered in an array of inspirational quotes on innovation and bravery (from Ghandi to Einstein and Yoda: 'Do or do not, there is no try'*). About 10 minutes before we were due to start, I popped my head out of the room and noticed a large number of attendees waiting outside the room looking decidedly nervous. I introduced myself and explained that the session ahead was going to be hard work but loads of fun and they didn't need to worry about a thing. It didn't seem to make a lot of difference. We ran the session and it was great. Everyone relaxed almost immediately and got involved from the word go. Afterwards, a couple of the attendees explained

* The Empire Strikes Back 1980

what the pre-workshop nerves were all about. They weren't afraid of us or our workshop. It was the room that gave them the collywobbles. Why? Because going to this seminar room had truly become something to fear. It was the place where all disciplinary hearings, tribunals, coaching sessions, redundancy announcements, tellings-off and other unpleasantries were delivered. It created a seriously negative association for everyone. However, by completely transforming the room's layout and adding some colour and theatre to the walls, their anxiety was immediately dissipated which allowed them to focus on the creative challenge ahead.

Don't underestimate the power of environment when it comes to releasing people's creativity and ideas.

Along with sorting out the layout of the room you'll need to supply everyone with some basic creative materials. We like to assemble creative boxes that the attendees can use in small groups throughout the session. For example, four creative boxes would be enough for 15 people. Each one has all the stuff they will need: pens and markers, Post-it® Notes, glue sticks, sticky tape, Blu-Tack®, scissors, coloured paper etc. If you want to go really crazy add pipe cleaners, fluffy balls, straws, lollipop sticks, gold stars and glitter. Feel free to use your imagination.

Provide a big supply of sweets and chocolates too. Some call them energy boosters; others say they're bribes to work hard. All we know is that everybody appreciates them and it gets things off to a great start.

Running the workshop
This is a flow chart you can use to shape the session.

Set up

↓

Framing

↓

Understanding Customers

↓

First Taste, First Thoughts, First Reactions

↓

Push Out Wide – Stimulus Injection

↓

Deepening – Colliding, Building & Theming

↓

Colliding, Building & Theming. Select & Hone

- ⊥ -

Colliding, Building & Theming Celebration

Step 1: Set up
Explain what you expect from people, how the session will feel and agree any rules on how you are going to behave with each other. Examples might include suspending your judgement of others' ideas, looking to build on ideas, stepping into the Stretch Zone, saying *and* not *but*, supporting your colleagues and being positive.

Step 2: Frame the challenge
Write your challenge in large letters on a flip chart, and define exactly what is meant by each word so everyone is clear. Capture comments on the flip chart so that by the end you have a complete and rich picture of what you are trying to achieve.

Step 3: Bring your customers into the room
Give each of your team a blank piece of paper and ask them to create a customer archetype. Help them to think of a typical

customer in the age bracket you have defined and ask them to write down a description of him or her, noting down as much as they can: their age, likes, dislikes, where they live, how they would describe themselves and so on. When that's done, ask them to draw a portrait of this person and really personalise them by giving them a name too.

Step 4: First Taste
This is the group's first taste of giving ideas so it's best to do it individually to get the ball rolling. Ask everyone to think of the first ideas that come into their heads and to write each idea down on a separate piece of paper (A5 card or paper is perfect) under two headings:

1. the idea headline (one line description like a newspaper headline);

2. the idea in a nutshell (a summary of how it works).

They should get their thoughts down quickly and not worry about how it looks or sounds.

Most people will have a number of ideas stored in their brain already, even if they are not aware of it, so this works as a download and clearing process ready for the next round.

When they've started drying up, get them into groups of four or five round the tables at the back of the room to share their ideas with each other.

Step 5: Stimulus injection #1 – into your customers' shoes
Ask everyone to get into pairs and share the customer archetypes they created earlier with each other. Staying in pairs they should generate new ideas (or build on the last round of ideas) by imagining they are truly in the shoes of those customers.

Thoughts should be captured on pieces of paper as before and then shared with the table.

Step 6: Stimulus injection #2 - looking to other worlds
Now it's time to have some fun and go a bit crazy. This is a great technique to get people thinking in a very different way.

This exercise requires a bit of advance effort from you but it's worth it. All you need to do is think of some different perspectives that would challenge your organisation's thinking and generate new and exciting ideas. For example: how would Apple approach your challenge and what ideas would they come up with? Or the British Army, John Lewis, Gordon Ramsay, Superman. The choice is yours. Think of about 30 different people or organisations and write one on a separate piece of paper.

With people still in their table groups, hand out a few of the names you've prepared to each group. Ask them to discuss what the traits of each person or organisation would be and then generate ideas from those perspectives. If they struggle with one let them move on to the next, but try to encourage them to think of at least one idea per group for each of the names they have. Capture the ideas in the same way.

Learning from other worlds is a wonderful tool that we use all the time. Last year we took a bunch of hospital porters to visit a huge Tesco superstore. Their pre-visit views were sceptical to say the least. After half a day in the superstore observing staff working and talking to managers, staff and customers it all became very clear to them. We ran an ideas session directly afterwards and the ideas they generated were amazing. And they amazed themselves: from how to order stock and store wheelchairs, to how to manage absence. They were inspired, and that was all to do with them experiencing something from a different perspective.

Step 7: The critical step – colliding, building and theming

You should have loads and loads of ideas by now, so ask the table groups to look through all their ideas and see if any join together or build on top of others to make bigger and better ideas. Once they have done that, get everyone in the room to lay their ideas on the floor and, as a group, try to collate them under different headings and themes. Keep the themes at quite a high level so you can really start to see where you have lots of interest and focus. You should now have a collated set of genius ideas lying on the floor in front of you.

Many people miss this step. Don't make the same mistake. It's about making sure the ideas are developed just that bit further so they have their rough edges knocked off and are enriched a little.

Step 8: Selecting

Now, it's time to focus on the most popular ideas and gauge the level of support for each. A great way to do this is to give each person five gold stars (or coloured dots) and explain they must read all the ideas carefully and allot their stars to their favourites – those that will have the most impact for customers and staff.

Once they've done this you will have a set of ideas that everybody has contributed to, so separate the top five and share them with the group. Repeat Step 7 now if you want, building on the ideas with the most stars so that they are really thought through.

Remember the art of leadership here, being positive about both the people and their output by congratulating everyone for generating some brilliant ideas that could make a huge difference to your business.

YOUR LEADERSHIP STYLE

While we are talking about leadership, we also want you to stand back from the process and think about how you need to *be* – your behaviours – as a leader throughout. You need to be a series of things: a role model, an encourager, a builder and a rewarder.

However, if you want to be slightly edgy as a leader, you also need to carefully plant a few ideas into the process: a radical one, a well-articulated one and a ridiculous one. It shows the team that all ideas are welcome. It also enables you to break the ice in terms of role-modelling as a creative risk taker.

In essence, what we have shown you here is what some people would refer to as a divergent-convergent ideas-building process. In leadership terms, this is a people-driven ideas process, which is a great signal to your team and others. If you choose to use this process as a longer-term approach, then there is room for some additional steps like observation and understanding. We would also recommend that you spend more time on Step 7 to really build up the ideas.

Implementation

Now you know how to deliver a great creative workshop and have a simple process to get your team thinking more creatively, you can use the process for this next step: how to get these ideas out in to the organisation so they work properly, staff are engaged and customers understand and appreciate them. In other words...implementation.

It's a word that puts dread into the heart of creative types as it means actually getting stuff done. It shouldn't be as scary as it is though, because the key to great implementation is to apply as much creativity (or more) to developing the implementation plan and approach as to generating the initial ideas and propositions. That means the creative process doesn't stop at the ideas phase; in fact it's only just the beginning.

Creative implementation is a book in itself, but let's focus on what we've discussed in this chapter. It sounds obvious, but ideas can be about anything. If you frame your challenge correctly and inject the right stimulus you can use your team to generate ideas at all stages of the innovation process, and that includes implementation.

The same workshop process described here can be applied to the creative implementation of your ideas. For example, going back to the workshop scenario, if one of your ideas had been to move products that older customers buy most to lower shelves, you could use this idea as stimulus for a workshop on engaging your teams in why doing this would be important. The implementation plan could include activities which truly engage the workforce in owning the change and wanting to make it happen, instead of just being told what to do. This is how real change occurs and, importantly, lasts.

So, to get the creative fires burning in your organisation you need to gauge the level of your innovation ambition, you need to give your people permission to be innovative within your agreed boundaries, and you need to have a process for harnessing their ideas. And you need to use your process throughout the cycle until your idea is out there and has become part of everyday life!

A FEW FINAL THOUGHTS:

- When you run your Zones exercise and creativity workshops you will notice a few leaders for innovation in your team – you know the type of people: first to pick up the pen, not afraid to step into the Stretch Zone, naturally creative and inspiring to their colleagues. We call these people Creative Champions. A really great way to kick start innovation in your area is to channel ideas from your wider team through Creative Champions so they are the face of creativity in the organisation. Get them running your workshops and encourage people to work together to develop ideas, and suddenly you'll have a groundswell of creativity that will grow exponentially.
- We haven't said who you should be getting ideas from. There's a simple answer to that – anyone and everyone.

key learning points

- Building on crossing the line in Chapter 3, think about how you get you and your team into a combined innovation Stretch Zone.
- Use this Stretch Zone to help you and your team find out who will run around the room naked to define your shared innovation ambition. You may need to revisit this over time to see if things are changing. If they aren't, why not?
- Identify how you can light creative fires in your team to get their creative juices going.
- Build and utilise a people-driven idea creation and building process you can be confident in. Don't leave it to chance.
- Be mindful about the type of ideas people lead with. How you respond to them will set a tone for how they perceive you as their leader. These ideas may need developing just that little bit further.

WORD CLOUD

chapter 6
spreading the word

At the beginning of the book, we mentioned that typing innovation into Google brings up millions of links. Randomly selecting pages in the list, it seems many of them talk about being able to develop more and more ideas across the organisation, which is a good thing. But the art of innovation is also about making innovation happen: implementing those newly designed concepts, getting them to market and squeezing every scrap of new value out of them.

The leader for innovation's challenge is not just about the relentless conception of new ideas and the drive to market; it's about building innovation capability across the organisation. That is, creating other innovation leaders, building innovation outside your own team, creating an environment to support widespread innovation and, importantly, getting innovation into the social fabric of the organisation.

It's easier said than done, though.

HOW ALIVE IS INNOVATION IN YOUR ORGANISATION?

An old colleague of ours was a specialist in building cell teams within manufacturing organisations. Whenever he went to work with a company, he'd spend the first few days just walking around and talking to people, to the frustration of the management. It wasn't the usual approach to interviews that the classical management consultants would take: instead he simply talked to all the people on the shop floor, in the offices, and importantly, in the car park (people always talk very frankly in the car park. Perhaps they think it isn't bugged).

He had a theory that if a company's reception area was full of plaques on quality management, Investors in People, mission statements and the like, nine times out of ten, no one knew anything about them, even though they walked past them every day.

He also used to say that he could tell the scale of the challenge in creating a team-based culture in the organisation in the first

30 seconds of being on site. His first and most enduring measure was if the car park had lots of spaces reserved for management. I'll leave you to decide which end of the scale he would put those companies.

dangerous quest

Before going any further, test the starting conditions for innovation across your organisation by completing a small, simple exercise. Don't worry, it's not too dangerous. Just make sure you're at work.

First, walk around the whole office building and look at the walls, team areas, café/restaurant, entrance, stairs, lifts, corridors, open areas, managers' desks, directors' rooms and desks (if you can – go on try), the toilets and even the store cupboards. Ask yourself whether you can see innovation happening, and to what extent innovation is being embraced. Now, if you're feeling brave, find a prominent area and put up some pictures of products or companies you think are innovative. Note what happens. Does anybody notice? Does anybody react? If they do, how long does it take before they ignore them again?

Second, talk to 10 people with whom you don't normally work, and ask them what they think was the last innovation to make it to market in your organisation. Why did they think it really was an innovation? Ask them who they thought was behind it.

Finally, ask the same people (or find some others if you're feeling adventurous):

- If you were to come up with something new and innovative what would happen?
- Who would take it forward for you (or not)?

- What would you need to do to get it going?
- Who would you need to sell it to, to make it go further?

If you are feeling really confident, write down your answers to these questions before you ask them, put them in an envelope, and then hide them. Gauge the answers or reactions you get (unscientifically of course) on a scale of 1 to 10: 1 being poor or vague, all the way to 10 for amazing.

The answer to these questions will give you an understanding of where you're starting from. If your answers are generally at the lower end of the range, then you may need to think very carefully about how much and how far you push people.

INNOVATION IN OTHERS

It's a nice feeling being the only leader for innovation in the organisation. People are always coming to you with, or for, ideas. It can also be a frustrating feeling: 'Am I the only one who gets this?', 'Come on let's do something different', or 'Why does it feel like everybody is against me?'. The crucial question is, if you are the only leader for innovation, what happens when you go on holiday?

The answer is, nothing. Even your team may struggle while you are away. This living, breathing organisation is not necessarily designed to allow people to be innovative without their innovation leader being present. It's a challenge, and it's also a risk.

As a leader of innovation and for innovation to flourish in the organisation, you need to do two things: 1) create other leaders for innovation, and 2) get innovation happening in other teams. There are a number of different approaches you can take depending on the challenge you face. Consider them as a part of your toolkit – some you can use in conjunction with others.

CREATING A SELF-SUSTAINING WAVE OF INNOVATION LEADERS

There is a natural group of colleagues who will be drawn to you, as an innovation leader. They will find your approach, style and energy engaging. They will ask themselves: 'Can I be like him/ her?' We believe that no matter what part of the organisation they come from, there is always scope for them to be innovation leaders to some degree.

Remember in Chapter 4 we talked briefly about the scale of innovation for new products and services. A similar scale also works for people's natural tendency to innovate. Psychologist Michael Kirton has developed a method called the Adaptor-Innovator Inventory which measures people's natural problem-solving style, adaptors are at one end and radical innovators are at the other. The further people are apart on this scale the harder it is for them to understand one another's approach to innovation.

case study

Take one of the world's largest shoe companies, designing and creating shoes for more than 40 countries, with design centres in five of them. For a couple of months, the global management team had been struggling to understand why they were losing ground to competitors at a local level. There were many reasons, and each team member had been asked to think about how they could use innovation to resolve the problems. However, when the management team came together they disagreed on the way forward. When asked about the scale of innovation that was needed, the divide became more acutely evident. The marketing and product director wanted to radically overhaul the entire range globally, with new styles, brands and packaging. The manufacturing director had a different view. It was more about the materials they were using, and their ability to switch products on or off that was going to be key. Each was equally valid. Each was at a different point on the scale. Once they understood that and why their perspectives where different, they could come together, discuss and agree.

Making waves

So how do you go about creating other innovation leaders? Do you hold a leaders' summit and get them all to change? Do you create a training course and tell them all to get on with it? Well, perhaps not yet. The way to think about creating innovation leaders is to think about waves.

This is about your colleagues, up and down the organisation, who have a relatively high degree of influence over what and how things are done, and the way in which people work. Think about who you can influence personally. They may be in your department, in your network across the organisation or people who joined the organisation at the same time as you and with whom you keep in touch. To see whether you do have influence over these people, consider whether they actively listen to you, seek your opinion, ask you to be involved in their projects or just ask you to talk to somebody for them now and again.

dangerous quest

Draw yourself on a piece of paper with the people you can influence around you, and then draw a ring around them. This is your personal sphere of influence. Within your sphere, certain leaders will have influence on leaders outside your sphere. As you identify them, you can draw circles around these groups too. This is your +1 or indirect sphere of influence. Within these +1 spheres, some of the leaders will again have influence on others totally outside any spheres you operate in. And so it goes on.

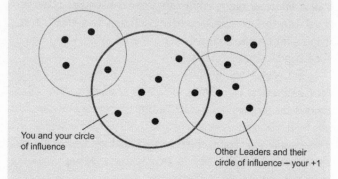

You and your circle of influence

Other Leaders and their circle of influence — your +1

By focusing on your personal sphere of influence, you can consciously act as an innovation leader role model, transferring knowledge and skills to other leaders through the act of doing. This will be your first wave of innovation leadership. In turn with your help and encouragement, you can enable this first wave of innovation leaders to influence those in the indirect spheres, repeating the process and creating new innovation leaders for themselves: your second wave.

The challenge from here is to make sure the waves continue, like a Mexican wave in a football stadium, as your level of influence and control diminishes. This is where some of the other tools in this chapter come to the fore, helping to inject energy, opportunities and activities to encourage the waves to continue.

Many people underestimate this human-centred level of change and don't think about how they can bring influence to bear. It is a component part of viral marketing: messages passed by trusted people, and at the same time encouraging them to adopt new ways of doing things. It's a very powerful approach to leader-led change.

Being a good role model

In an earlier chapter we touched on role modelling with respect to you and your team, and to some extent the principles here are the same. Being a role model means demonstrating to fellow leaders how to be innovative on a personal level and how to encourage innovation in others.

To get you going, here are a few simple things you can do. For those feeling more adventurous, you can apply some of the ideas in the Go Guerrilla section in Chapter 7.

- Invite and induct fellow leaders on to a review panel with you, for a project that one of your team is working on and that contains a high level of innovation.
- Involve them in one of your creativity sessions and then go through what happened and why.
- Ask them to organise and deliver a creativity event with you, in either your or their area of the organisation, again making sure you put time in after the event to work through their experiences.
- Tell them you have had a complete mental block trying to overcome a challenge and you need their help to solve it.
- Compliment them whenever you see creative behaviour.
- Ask them to do you a favour that will require some leadership through innovation. Say you owe them some creativity favours with respect to their challenges.
- Ask them to stand in for you at a conference on innovation (internal or external), so they have to learn the content from you and understand how to deliver it.

And lastly, these are a bit stretching but can help focus the mind:

- Ask for help on some radical issues, e.g. say all your jobs are at risk if you don't come up with some new joint ideas on an important board issue by the end of the week.

- Paint a picture of the future that needs some radical innovation, such as legislation change that's going to need a reduction in the workforce by 50 per cent, the merger of three business areas or increasing revenue by reducing the number of products/services by 25 per cent.
- Leave a report summary lying around that says competitors are pushing innovation in the next year and your company could be hit if it doesn't do something now.

SEEDING INNOVATION INTO OTHER TEAMS

If creating innovation leaders seems like a hard first step, then you can try to seed innovation in other teams first. This is challenging as you don't yet have leaders on board to support you. However, within your sphere of influence, you should be able to find supporters who can and will help.

There is some conventional wisdom in business around building and spreading capability, with merits and dangers to each. These are:

Convention #1: Shuffle the deck

This is the philosophy of moving people around to diffuse innovation among wider groups or teams of people. It is often a reason why seemly high-performing teams often get disbanded. There are dangers with this approach. Just moving people around with no support or transition and expecting innovation to just happen doesn't work. Worryingly, it's a method some leaders use when they actually want to *stop* change happening too – but more on that later.

Convention #2: Support the new way by promoting the pioneers

We see this scenario frequently: people are promoted to new and higher positions across a company, whether or not they have demonstrated any leadership or management capabilities and behaviours. From these new positions it is expected that they will continue to get results, while being given difficult challenges to resolve and teams to lead. It's a version of the Peter Principle where people are promoted to their level of incompetence.

The concept of seeding is different. It's about planting appropriate seeds in a team and then helping them germinate until they get to a point where they can grow on their own. The challenge with conventional approaches is that they focus on sowing and don't always support the germination period.

Seeding teams can be achieved in many ways. In our experience the most effective are:

1. picking one or two people from your team and getting them involved in other projects in other departments, with the specific aim of transferring skills to their colleagues;

2. rotating people from other teams into your team for a period of time so that they absorb your different ways of working before moving back to their original team.

Either way, you need to focus on your area of the business first: you understand the projects and can identify those that need innovation injecting into them. Try to pick those that are driven by your part of the organisation, but also cut across other areas. You need buy-in from other managers to get the bandwidth from them to give it a go, relying on their trust and the value they see in innovation. If you've managed to develop new innovations and get them to market or release value from them, this won't be hard.

It's really important to identify a variety of projects with different levels of difficulty and duration. The challenge is not to take on too much too quickly, as you'll end up running headlong into the conventional approach of splitting up your team and moving them around. As you focus on germinating the seeds, make sure that any person you second from your team is capable of developing others through action learning.

SET-UP IS EVERYTHING

Before people are placed with projects or others are brought in, you need to go through a considered set-up process. Sit down with your team and explain the approach and plan: how they will demonstrate innovation, transfer skills and adopt the right behaviours. Finally, make sure there is a safety net for them in case things don't quite go to plan.

Any person who comes into your team(s), and those you have seconded to other projects, are all working for you. Support and coaching are vital to their and your own future success.

INNOVATION AS A CONSCIOUS, SOCIAL MOVEMENT

Put 'Black Eyed Peas', 'I've Gotta Feeling' and 'Oprah Winfrey' into YouTube and watch the video. This is a famous clip of how a group of enthusiastic people can lead and seed a wave of change. It works by taking some volunteers, around 800 of them, training them in both the dance moves, the change plan and how to encourage people, and then strategically placing them in the crowd. As the song runs on, the pre-trained dancers start to come in, encouraging others around them, energetically showing them what to do, and over the course of the song getting everybody (as many as 30,000 people) to join in.

It's a living, breathing example of the change a few people can make with a mass of people around them. In the business world, it can't be that easy, can it? Why not?

We often refer to these social drivers for change as firelighters: people who are natural innovators, are spread across the organisation and can develop into role models for others. In our book about customer service we wrote about the role of service firelighters. The principles we discussed there are roughly the same.

Unlike service, innovation is not always infectious. It can be seen as fun, exciting and liberating. It can also be seen as risky and slightly unnerving for many. Therefore, the challenge of finding and inducting people into a firelighter role might be more daunting than you initially think. You also need to be acutely aware that just because people are naturally innovative, it doesn't necessarily mean that they will be good at passing on the message.

If you or your team don't know them already, the ideal people can be spotted with the help of a few well-chosen activities. Refer to the Go Guerrilla section in Chapter 7 for some ideas. The next step is to develop these firelighters. To do this you need:

- your innovation approach and toolkit;
- a safe space where you can work;
- methods for practising and building new skills, e.g. case examples, simulations, actors for role play;
- an appropriate amount of time, and;
- an ongoing plan for development.

a little illustrative example

Early in the reign of Greg Dyke at the BBC, there were a number of organisational development programmes. One was called 'Inspiring Creativity Everywhere'. In BBC Resources, a former commercial business under the BBC umbrella, they decided to develop a small virtual team of innovation 'representatives' as firelighters, with the remit to support others in developing their ideas and creating innovative solutions and services for their customers. They quietly took 25 hand picked people out of the organisation for two two-day sessions, and through a three-part process trained them to become innovation representatives. The first part of the process was the *doing* element of this role, bringing out their collective understanding of innovation and instilling new thinking, tools and approaches to supplement their capability, through mini-simulations of projects. The second part was focused on *being*, enabling them to develop their coaching approach and behaviours in a safe and supportive environment. The final part of the process was to introduce them to the organisation where, in the first instance, they just offered their support to friendly colleagues, who talked to them about their innovation challenges. This controlled the first taste these guys had of their role, in a manner designed to increase their confidence.

The brilliance of this approach was that there was no fanfare to promote these firelighters across the organisation. The firelighters focused on talking and coaching others around innovation, enabling them to initiate and keep innovation thriving through others, rather than taking over and doing it for them.

The net effect of this type of change can be seen in the Black Eyed Peas video. Slowly but surely the virtual team encourage others to be increasingly innovative, raising innovation across the whole organisation. But social movements can take time and many people have written very big books on it. If you want to speed it up, read on.

A COUPLE OF TECHNIQUES THAT WILL GIVE YOU MORE BANG FOR YOUR BUCK

In many years of bringing about change in organisations, we have developed a couple of techniques that really help to speed up the pull towards change.

The first is creative engagement, which is about appealing to your audience on a variety of levels so that you can attract their attention in the workplace. The second is called Go Guerrilla. It's about going underground and doing things that create either the opportunity for, or an atmosphere around, innovation.

Each seeks to boost the potential for innovation across the organisation.

GETTING CREATIVITY IN THE ENGAGEMENT OF OTHERS

You probably already manage the stakeholders in your organisation, by framing the information you need them to digest in an appropriate way. However, stop and think for a minute. How many of those stakeholders are truly engaged beyond the moment of the initial pitch? Does longer lasting change often fail because stakeholders are not enticed by that first contact?

One reason for the failure of change is that people lose connection with that change and almost run out of energy during it. In most organisations today there's always so much going on, with increasing numbers of communication channels (including email, the biggest communication-disabling medium going). Getting your message through the rest of the noise is a big challenge.

Experience tells us that in order to truly engage an individual you have to convince them of more than just the rational business benefits. You have to grab their attention on a number of levels and appeal to them as human beings. This means being creative in your approach and standing out from the crowd whilst not diluting your message: putting a naked person on the front of your project material may get you noticed, but may not do much for the credibility of your project, or your reputation for that matter (and yes, we know somebody who did this).

We also heard a story about creative engagement concerning a well-known supermarket. They wanted to raise the profile of internal initiatives across their stores. So they created a pilot of

Staff-TV, an internal channel beamed securely over a satellite network channel, with staff making programmes for their colleagues. In one edition, they gave a video camera to staff in a store with a really good health and safety (H&S) record and asked them to create a short video to highlight H&S issues. It was such a success that it was rumoured that there was a reduction in health and safety related issues by as much as 65 per cent across the whole store network.

This story highlights the importance of getting creativity into the process through your staff, or as a tool to aid your staff. Remember that through their spheres of influence, staff will be able to promote ideas or build bridges with others around the organisation, helping to create that wave.

Of course, the greater the creativity, the greater the opportunities for engaging the rest of the organisation, top to bottom, side to side, even underground.

key learning points

- Win over other leaders to your way of thinking by demonstrating the value of the innovation, and the opportunities it creates.
- Mastermind and bring about change in a series of waves, each orchestrated to build energy and momentum as you go. Start with people and win them over, one person at a time.
- Consider how you use your team to seed innovation in other areas and other teams, but don't be seduced into splitting them up or disbanding them.
- Don't fall into the 'same old same old' trap. Get creative about how you engage others.

WORD CLOUD

chapter 7
go
guerrilla

Have you spotted this shopping phenomenon? On high streets across the country there are small, high fashion brands popping up in warehouse-style stores for just a few weeks, only to disappear again as quickly as they appeared. Their aim is to swoop in, make an impact, sell to everybody they can as quickly as they can, then get out. Brilliant. They are based on the observation that most shops make a killing in the first few weeks of being open because they are new, fresh and exciting. They also play on that part of the human psyche that is compelled to act by the impression of limited availability, 'if I don't get it now...' The additional benefit of moving them around is that they reach people they wouldn't normally, not even via the Internet. One retail analyst once referred to them lovingly as guerrilla shops. Now they are more commonly known as pop-up shops. We once tried to talk a colleague at a large high street department store chain into trying them as a way of reaching into smaller, but desirable towns. Maybe one day.

SUBTLE ENCOURAGEMENT

As a tool for supporting innovation and innovation leadership across the organisation, Go Guerrilla works in the same way: carefully designed activities that pop up under the radar, last a few minutes, hours or days and then disappear. The aims of Go Guerrilla are to stimulate people and activate the grapevine; create a culture more open to innovation; enable potential leaders to get a simple first taste of innovation in a non-threatening way; encourage people to be a little more innovative without them even realising it (until of course you point it out to them) and work within low budgets.

One of the best stories we have heard on the guerrilla theme comes from a small high technology manufacturer. They design, manufacture and supply parts to Formula One (F1) teams. They were in the middle of a big culture change programme and were worried that they were losing the support of some highly skilled employees.

In order to convert a few of the cynics who were very influential in the business, the MD arranged for one of them to visit a customer. He chose an operative who worked on a machine manufacturing a critical part, was very experienced and was often involved in the design process. 'Bloody hell. Why me?' was the response. What he didn't know was that the MD had talked with the customer about him, his capability and why he was critical to the process. The customer sent the operative to the test track, where he met the F1 team, and went round the track in a sports car at 150 mph. He was then taken to the design centre where they talked about the new design work. He even joined a design review and found that he could contribute to it, based on his own experience and knowledge of his company's work. He returned to work full of stories and with renewed passion. Most importantly, the experience had reinforced his understanding of the need for change.

REMEMBER: STRETCH ZONE

When using the guerrilla approach, it is important to make sure that nobody is put in harm's way. By that we mean is made to feel vulnerable, or pushed well outside their Stretch Zone into panic; it will soon backfire on you. This doesn't mean you can't be utterly creative or even dangerous. One last thing; take great care with suggestion box schemes. These are not guerrilla-type activities. As an aside we think many of these types of schemes are fruitless because they are often unsupported, used in ways that hinder collaboration, and have a negative reputation. In America I have heard that they often refer to these as 'garbage can systems', because 99 per cent of the outcomes from them are rubbish.

dangerous quest

Try this guerrilla alternative to the suggestion box. Think of a simple challenge you, your team or your customers face day to day. Just a simple one. Now, put on a sandwich board and walk up and down the office. As you do, encourage people to get their ideas onto paper and stick them onto you. You'll be surprised at how many suggestions you'll get.

We have found that guerrilla activities are usually about doing small and clever things often; little things that on their own don't feel like they add up to much, but put together raise the noise level.

Here are a few things you can do, some of which we have seen in other companies, arranged by level depending on your ambition.

Simple and straightforward
- Introduce a five minute ideas session on a hot topic into every, yes *every*, meeting you run.
- At stand-up every morning with your team (see Chapter 4), introduce a creative activity, e.g. rate how you are feeling on a scale of 1 to 10, or if you were a colour today which one you would be? Just simple things that prompt creativity (of course you will need to explain this carefully). Then when others join your team, they will start doing it.
- Rename all projects to sound more innovative (a favourite of FMCG R&D teams already, but in their case often for secrecy reasons).
- Find and print information about innovative thinking and put it in all the coffee areas and in reception, but don't leave it there too long.
- Put inspirational quotes and pictures of inspirational leaders around the building, especially on the ceilings.
- Slowly take away everyday things, e.g. insist that present-ations to the management team are done without PowerPoint; use voice files rather than written documents, etc.

- Ask people to speak in the language of a six-year-old with a strict ban on using the usual company jargon.
- On a sunny day, run a meeting outside on the grass.
- Ask people in your team, and network, to go and visit innovative stores when they are out shopping at the weekend. But make sure you capture and discuss their experiences and observations on the following Monday.
- Become a living archetype of a customer for a day. Encourage a few of your fellow leaders to do the same, so that it sets an example of getting into the mindset and shoes of your customers.
- Get people to sit in a different place each day.

Needs a little more thought

- Take over the canteen at lunchtime and run a gallery of new innovations that are out in the market, asking people for thoughts and opinions on whether these innovations will be a hit or a miss (make sure you include a few ridiculous ones).
- Organise a session for new companies to come in to pitch their products and services via a set of walk-in briefings in a large meeting room.
- Bring in a local recognised charity and invite people to come to a session to help them think of new ideas to generate money (and of course make sure everybody gives a bit too).
- Take over one lift and turn it into an ideas development lab, asking anybody who gets in to contribute one idea before they leave.
- Set up a video pod and ask people to go in and tell a story of something innovative they have done in their roles in this, or their previous, company. Have the video edited (by a media studies student if you don't have any in-house help) and run it in reception, on the intranet or at the next management meeting.

- Take over a wall, hire an artist for the afternoon and create a storyboard about a recent project, or feedback from customers, and invite people to comment on it. Take it down a couple of days later.
- Organise and run a market stall over a lunchtime that offers to teach people a new creative tool in exchange for their ideas on a problem.
- Systematically take over the coffee machines or social areas (one day to the next) with big foam boards or flip chart pads. Put on some light music to change the atmosphere, and invite people to write ideas or opinions about how the environment supports or restricts innovation in the company.
- Put boards in your business area labelled 'innovation behaviours and values'. Start acknowledging those who have demonstrated desired behaviours by sticking notes on the boards to say who it was and what they did. Encourage your team to do the same and then invite others to join in. Then you have a choice about personally rewarding those with the most feedback with a nice little something to show it matters.
- Buddy people up to job-swap for a day. Give them a tight brief: they must look at each others' roles and see how they could make them more creative. If you can, get people from the back office to do it with people in the front, so they get very different experiences.
- Identify and establish a couple of customers as expert customers. Ask them to be more challenging with staff about the solutions they want, in order to provoke more innovative behaviours from them.
- Create a group of staff from customer-facing roles across the company to be the voice of the customer in meetings at all levels of decision-making.

- Use your own product to create some novel furniture for meeting rooms (the Top Gear factor).

Imagination required

- Send some of the lead people a creative gift, anonymously of course. You can always be clever and arrange for them all to hold bits of a bigger puzzle that only comes together when they speak to each other about it.
- Ask IT to install a new Internet browser favourites list on fellow leaders' PCs, with links to creativity and innovation papers, interesting facts and things to stimulate. They will eventually find it whilst using their browser.
- Approach the latest crop of new joiners, brief them individually on a creative challenge, but tell them not to tell anybody. Then let them go. It's a mini secret innovator wave.
- Another idea for new joiners is to ask them to come to the company a week before their start date to be a mystery shopper. It's a great way of getting insight and also sheep-dipping them in the company environment.
- On the bottom of circular emails, add a special invite to people to come to a secret location to take part in a visioning activity, but tell them not to announce it. The people who read it will be the only people allowed to come.
- Try giving themes to some areas of the office, e.g. meeting rooms could be the customer room, the thinkers' room, the risk takers' room, the pit-stop room (only allowed to book it for five minutes). Anything that creates a different atmosphere.
- Lastly...and we know companies don't like their employees doing this out of their control so think carefully about it... set up a false company on Twitter and get people from your company to tweet, saying what they are doing that day that is innovative, supports innovation or may result in innovation.

MAKE IT POWERFUL

You know, somebody once said to us that they had a go at this type of guerrilla activity in their organisation. Apparently, the management team decided to run some 'Dragon's Den' style workshops to try to showcase the company's changing attitude towards creativity and innovation and demonstrate that they were open to new ideas. They thought it was a guerrilla activity because it felt like a trendy thing to do. The thing is, if something is widely publicised as a management activity, is it a guerrilla activity? Possibly not.

Remember, Go Guerrilla can be a very powerful method for influencing people and creating an atmosphere of innovation as an under-the-radar type activity. To make it really powerful, think of it as a campaign, where you use activities like those above as tools over a period of time to change attitudes and behaviours towards innovation. To be incredibly effective you need to apply some good old fashioned innovation theory and be very clear about your audience – which groups, where, what are they like, etc.? This will enable you to figure out which guerrilla activities to use so you stretch them carefully and in a very conscious way.

If you get it right, the effects can be amazing, lasting and ultimately very effective.

key learning points

- Go Guerrilla is about doing things under the radar to slowly bring about or to activate change.
- Think little and clever. Identify all the little things you can do that can encourage creativity and innovation.
- Think small, and 'pop up' is also the best way to go.
- Build a simple campaign to help you plan and bring about change over time.

WORD CLOUD

chapter 7³⁄₄

you, your organisation and the physical environment

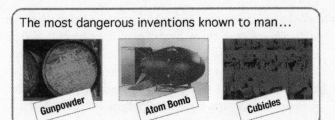

The most dangerous inventions known to man...

Gunpowder

Atom Bomb

Cubicles

hhhhh. Don't tell a soul. This is a short secret chapter. It's because it contains the best kept secret in the world; that the physical environment is one of the biggest enablers of both leadership and innovation you can ever tap into. It's also a big and lasting signal.

Now we've said it, it might sound obvious. But actually it's the one thing that is the easiest to change, yet it is often the one thing left to chance. By and large we take it for granted, except, say, for a whiteboard, a few framed pictures and some nice desks. And what's worse, we often hand it over to people in facilities management with no guidance, except financial or health and safety, on what to do. But if we change our approach to the environment and involve people like those in facilities management, we can think more freely about how the environment can make a real and lasting impact. Suddenly, you will see their eyes light up.

For example, the facilities team in GlaxoSmithKline see themselves as critical in creating employee engagement in the organisation. Their strategy is to create an environment that wows people so they want to join the company when they come for interviews; an environment that people want to be in and work in, day in day out; an environment that is a major reason for people wanting to stay if they are headhunted to leave.

JOINING THE CULTURE CLUB

Many innovative organisations don't talk about their environment. It's just there. Yet they've taken the time to really invest in it, to make it work. There are some brilliant examples, and it's all about how far you want to go. Within five minutes of walking into any organisation, from the environment alone you should be able to get a sense of what the culture is like, what it means to people, what is happening where and how supportive it is.

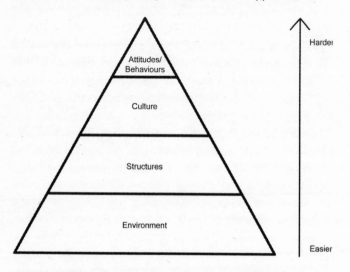

And you know, it's actually quite simple. It takes just a bit of effort but can have the biggest impact. If there's money to spend, make sure it's used wisely. Don't leave it to the PA and the office stationery catalogue. That's the lazy answer.

If there's no budget, pilot some new ideas and then link them to any refresh or major change. O2's new headquarters is built next to their old one. The Employee Involvement and Facilities teams worked together to design and pilot some new schemes within their existing environment, so they could take them into their new one. They tried new working areas; looked at office-based and mobile working and how they could be supported more effectively; experimented with a variety of meeting room formats; brought in a selection of different chairs and desks and had different people (the unusual suspects like security) try them and they designed different wall schemes, and tried new approaches to communication. They included a whole host of pilots to find the best combinations. They even talked some of the management team into working from different places around the building. By virtue of careful planning and design, most new ideas were an out and out success and were incorporated into the new building. It's a great expression of the business and its culture. It's also a testament to their appetite for innovation.

Every time you are out visiting different organisations (especially if you think they are particularly innovative) observe what their environment is like, what could you take back and make work in your organisation.

dangerous quest

Here's a little list of places to go and experience some innovation environments:

- Pixar's HQ on the second DVD of the brilliant *Monsters Inc.*
- The Science Museum in London.
- Type the following in different combinations into your search engine and click the images section (of course, make sure you have your content filters on, just in case things have changed since we last looked at them):
  - 'innovative workspaces'
  - 'creative studios'
  - 'innovation centres'
  - 'concept design studio'
  - 'creative meeting spaces'

And a few specific ones:
- ° 'P&G innovation centres'
- ° 'GSK innovation hubs'
- ° 'Lego® design spaces'
- ° 'inside Microsoft's HQ'
- ° 'Royal Mail Innovation Lab'

And for something really different:
- ° A book: *Big Ideas – Small Buildings* by Phyllis Richardson (Thames and Hudson), 2007.

If you are really stuck, go to our website, send us an email and we will send you a few choice pictures of stimulating environments we have seen.

START SMALL

We have worked on loads of programmes where we've changed the environment within an organisation to make it more supportive of innovation and much more engaging to work in. We've often taken a *start small* approach and found that it works. Here's a simple five-step approach to get you going:

1. Small team, small investigation

Avoid a direct cut-and-paste idea. It won't fit or match who you are, what you do now or would like to do in the future. As an example, many outpatient departments in NHS Trusts use a ticket-based queuing system that was first seen at deli counters in supermarkets. On the surface it's a good idea. It works in supermarkets up to a point. But in an environment where there are multiple consultation rooms, multiple appointments, and multiple queues, it often leaves people rooted to the spot with their ticket, panicking about whether they might miss their slot. It worked in one environment and then it was copied, but somehow the idea got lost in translation.

Follow good design principles, and use what you see as stimulus to help you design the right approach for you. Think of the environment as a service. Now get out there and go and see what others do; other companies, agencies, flagship shops, factories, museums, coffee houses, airport lounges and even parks. Take a small team. Do it short, sharp and land it well.

Once you've done that, look around your place and go into observation mode. What's happening, where? What's not happening, and why? What's the environment saying to you? Does it feel innovative? For example, does everybody sit at their own desks with dividers between them, in rows with their backs to each other, creating barriers to talking? Or do desks stay vacant when people are out of the office? If people sit with their backs to each other and the conversation is mute, you could install those long Viking-style tables we talked about earlier. It will help them talk about the work they are doing. Of course, some will say that certain environments are a distraction, so create some quiet areas that people can work in when necessary.

2. Activate the senses

Now you have tried a few things and are a bit more confident, get a small group together and develop a five-senses vision for the environment, to act as a catalyst and guide for anything you design. If you want to get buy-in to this vision, involve people in reviewing and revising it in a gallery-style way, in corridors, or in meetings; anywhere that they can feel they've contributed. It can generate support too.

3. Design

The next step is to identify some things you can do as a pilot and design them with the team and anybody related to the pilot areas. Imagine, if you can, that the environment is a service to people. It will help in the design. You have a choice here. You can focus on the little things that will boost creativity and innovation in your teams, such as supporting some of the activities in this book, or you could go the whole hog and redesign a complete area or two.

For example, if there are no meeting *rooms*, think meeting *spaces*. They don't have to be permanent structures, they could be like booths in a restaurant. How about using colour to signal a change from one area to another? A single coloured wall might be enough. How about putting up banners to signal which team is which, with their names, photos and key challenges on them?

If getting out is hard, bring some art/design/architecture students in and ask them to do it for you. We tried this approach in a project with Nottingham Business School. They were moving to a new building and wanted to redesign the lecturers' environment to make it more supportive, and to help them demonstrate academic leadership. We involved a few architecture students and gave them a very simple brief: to help us find and develop some examples as stimulus to put into the project. It was a great success as the students came up with ideas we would never have thought of, right down to taking the covers off infamous business books and turning them into transparent floor tiles, to create the impression of 'walking on knowledge'. If you try this approach, ask people for examples of things that they feel have been successful in the companies in which they've previously worked.

4. Go and try a few things
...and then of course get them built and try them out, but for a limited time. If you have to, do it in your area first, but don't forget to get others to experience them too. Capture and build feedback as you go. But avoid at all cost it becoming something that only innovative people can use. Otherwise you risk turning it into another thing that people either think is exclusively theirs, or, something that people just don't want or refuse to use.

5. Pilots to permanent

Changes to the environment often have a way of becoming permanent without the need for formal reviews, Senior leaders see them and like them, other areas start to follow suit so if you don't need to have a formal review then great.

However, if you do undertake a formal review then make sure that it is balanced. You might need to build a case for whole company change, so link it to any strategic imperatives that you can. You might not need to of course; if you get to here, it's pretty unusual for it to fail.

This was only a brief chapter to get your juices going. We plan to write a short book on this. If you want to contribute let us know. Good luck! And of course, keep the secret.

chapter 8
Priming your innovation catapult

Our assumption is that if you are reading this, then you have at least taken your first step. And to paraphrase a famous saying: from one small step from you, comes one huge leap for innovation, for your team and for your organisation. But what happens if you don't have time to take small steps; if all around you people are crying out for innovation but don't know it yet? What you need is something that will propel your organisation's innovation with the right pace and with some degree of certainty. There will be risks as well as barriers, and your programme needs energy and momentum.

What you need is an *innovation catapult*.

FINDING YOUR INNOVATION CATAPULT

Simon's dad once gave him a picture that he kept on the wall. To him it perfectly depicted the issue of getting innovation into an organisation. The picture was of a group of knights in front of a castle going into battle. They were brandishing all the usual knightly trappings: swords, shields, and armour. The enemy was similarly equipped. Behind one of the knights stood an inventor, who was tapping on his shoulder and pointing to a Gatling gun to his left. The knight was most perturbed at the interruption and glanced back shouting 'NOT NOW! DON'T YOU SEE I HAVE A BATTLE TO WIN?'.

It's a pretty apt picture. In the heat of the moment, we often miss the things that give us the edge, the leap forward, the advantage; we stick to what we know, and why not? It seems to have worked in the past.

The picture also showed the difficulty of changing people's behaviour towards something new. It highlighted the challenge of standing back, taking a moment to spot what will get you where you want to be: your catapult. Below you'll see just a few possibilities.

The piggy-back

Let's start with the old favourite of the serial piggy-backers:

spotting and using change in the organisation to propel ideas forward. This is a favoured change approach of advertisers, who are quick to spot new social movements and to jump on board to bring about change in favour of the products they promote. Civil servant, Sir Humphrey Appleby, used this approach to get what he wanted from his 'supposed' boss, PM Jim Hacker, in the British comedy classic, *Yes, Prime Minister*.

We have talked about some of this in Chapter 6, and you will probably have experienced this type of catapult before, so we won't dwell on it here. However, the trick for you as a leader is to link your desired programme or outcomes to whatever wave is rolling though your organisation. Piggy-back on it, attract some of the profile and resources and showcase some of your innovation leadership capabilities.

For example, in many implementation-strong organisations like Tesco, there is a clearly defined set of strategic programmes that lead the implementation of new initiatives across the organisation. The key to implementation is to link your programme to one of these. By doing this, you make sure your project is strategically aligned, which means you also avoid the risk of having it shut down.

Just one word of warning: you'll have to figure out how to combine the benefits of the two programmes so they are seen as one, otherwise it's a pretty obvious steal.

If this is the tried and trusted way, what other, more stretching ways of catapulting are there?

Compelling external force

We once hired a researcher to look into how new innovations travel through organisations and make it to market. We were interested in understanding whether an initial idea, one that was strong and compelling enough, could make it through an organisation on its own merit, or whether some inspired genius had to fight to keep it going. The results showed that it depended largely on the organisation and the relative importance of the programme to which the innovation related. It also showed the importance of leaders keeping the intent of the innovation in the minds of the team, to stop it being eroded away (the sausage machine).

There was an important by-product of that research. Many innovation-led companies, like 3M, employ a front door and back door innovation structure. If you don't get your idea through the front door, you can use something called your personal innovation time allowance (3M being the original pioneers of this concept) to develop it through the back door. This back door method is the focus of our story.

case example

A small group of innovation leaders used their personal development time to develop a new product which showed up grease and moisture on car panels prior to respraying. It was new and very different, but it didn't conform to the front door approach as it didn't sit on any product plan or sales strategy. So they developed the product with a potential customer who had a clear need for it. To do this, they begged help from their colleagues in manufacturing to set up a small pilot plant with existing kit, started to make some small production runs and with the help of the customer, tested and honed the product. That customer told their own clients and partners, and, so the story goes, a sales director at the company got a call from a field agent asking to buy a pallet of the new product to sell in his local market. He had customers asking for it, even though it wasn't on any sales list. The Sales Director, of course, didn't know anything about the product, but a sale is a sale. Within a couple of years it was their biggest seller in that market.

This is a pretty extreme example, but it demonstrates the power of an external force, like customer desire or the risk of losing out to the competition. The latter drives many a director nuts.

If you're going to take this approach here are some things to think about:

- List all the external forces you can think of: customers, competitors, regulation, partners, corporate social responsibility, etc. Include new products on the fringes of what your company offers, so not just direct competitors.
- Think through which offer opportunities for you to kick-start innovation, without risking long-term opportunities. For example, can you get an existing, friendly customer onside, without putting the company or its strategy at risk?
- For those that are left, think about how you can push them forward with a little bit of innovation, effort and leadership.
- Finally, can you use this to catapult innovation without glorifying yourself too quickly?

The last one might sound counterintuitive. Why do something if you are not going to receive some praise, reward or recognition in return? The challenge is to avoid getting the recognition too early. It can raise your profile too quickly, placing you under the scrutiny of others. Unless, of course, you have the culture in your organisation to support it.

Go off-piste

Going off-piste is just as it sounds: spotting something on the fringe of the company that people are already involved in who might have the ear of an executive.

Companies are always trying to figure out how they can improve quality, reduce cost, boost teamwork, or increase cohesiveness across the organisation. These are perfect projects to support and turn into catapults.

Did we just say reduce costs?

Cost-reduction projects are of course an interesting quandary for innovators: they can provide a perfect opportunity for embedding innovation because the traditional way of approaching cost reduction is to think of it as a sausage too, from which you can slice of the percentage you want.

Cost-cutting projects should always be approached from an innovation perspective. However, the mere fact that it's cost reduction sends a shiver up the spine of most people.

So ask the management team to let you drive an alternative project that's in competition with the traditional approach. This gives you the opportunity to show that innovation can help and get it on the agenda of people around the organisation.

STEADY LEADS TO DANGEROUS

We're getting you on the road to being more dangerous, but here are some other ways to create spark, energy and dazzle, and give you a slightly dangerous edge:

- Take over the annual company conference and do it in an innovative way. Alternatively, take over the annual AGM with investors. Both require significant investment in time, energy and stakeholder management.
- A more dangerous approach to using external forces would be to use the rumour or threat of a new, powerful competitor in your market as a catapult for innovation. For example, the threat of Tesco entering the UK financial services market reverberated through the industry, well before the company actually decided to do it.
- An alternative, but just as dangerous, use of external forces would be to pursue green technologies in a big way, convincing the organisation that this is an innovative way forward.
- Try working with the unions or shared service providers, such as cleaners, security, etc. Get innovation into contracts with

HR or IT. This may sound more difficult than it is; companies often ask for innovation in such contracts, but fail to define and measure it. This is a great opportunity for those brave enough to try. It doesn't have to relate to the whole contract; focus on an element of innovation that will benefit an aspect of the contract, or a section of the organisation.

● Jump on something very opportune in the organisation, such as the creation of a new unit, new team or even a new building. It's a chance to start with a blank piece of paper, keep it out of the existing business structures and rules, and use it as a catapult to demonstrate the potential of innovation. Of course, you will need to go out on a limb, but the possibilities are enormous, especially if you can get authorisation to treat it like a pilot area of the business.

● Look at new acquisitions in the same way. They come with baggage and expectations, but new acquisitions can bring with them managers keen to demonstrate their value. They are keen to try new things and are open to new ideas. It's not easy to get involved and persuade management of the opportunity; it can depend on the rationale behind the acquisition. It's worth a try though, if you are willing to take the risk.

TO LAUNCH OR NOT TO LAUNCH...

A great person once said that it's better to ask forgiveness afterwards than to wait for permission. In terms of innovation, we totally agree.

We frequently meet or hear of people who are waiting for the signal from others to start leading. If you wait or ask, you risk the chance of getting a no. And as many a graveyard of failed leaders will tell you, once you get a no, there's no going back. Think of the great courtroom battle in the film *A Few Good Men*, where the character played by Demi Moore repeatedly asks the judge to change his mind. Annoyed, he repeatedly reaffirms his position and won't change his mind. It's the same principle; no matter how the argument is played out, there is no coming back from a no.

So, we always advocate working within the sphere of the permission that you already have, or asking for just enough permission to get you so far. Don't put yourself in such a position that you set yourself up for a complete no.

Similarly, we recommend avoiding big announcements and launches. It sends a signal to the organisation to prepare its defences, or highlights a target that might need taking down a peg or two. It can also encourage initiative fatigue.

We prefer a slightly more subtle approach, as you have seen; one that is slightly underground and somewhat guerrilla in outlook. It's a three-step approach to getting things going:

1. Don't launch just do
With enough self-taken permission to get you going, but not enough to cut your throat. It's all about getting innovation leadership into action, just one step at a time.

2. Soft launch
Quietly launching an innovation to a few chosen people, in order to signal to them that they have permission to proceed and an opportunity to get things working.

3. Hard launch
The bigger bang launch, with a fanfare, backed with some well-won results that are indisputable.

It's an approach we have used time and time again. It may not be dangerous, but it definitely works.

A CHALLENGE SHARED IS A CHALLENGE OVERCOME
Before we go any further, here's a health warning. There is a group of people out there whom you never know to avoid until

it's too late. We are not talking about the grenade-lobbing, highly vocal cynics. They're subtly different. We are talking about people who are tricky to spot, even though they are characterised by an inability to stand up and be counted. We find the following illustration helps to separate them out.

Positive

Window Shoppers:
Talk a good talk,
and prefer to keep talking

Passion Activists:
Very positive and
proactively motivated

Paralysed ———————————————— **Active**

Happy Day'ers:
Moan, and happy to keep
moaning about anything

Resistant Fighters:
Actively do anything to keep
things the way they are

Negative

The group we are talking about are not to be confused with the moaners, who are themselves inactive but very easy to spot. These Happy Day'ers seem to be happy just to moan. They moan about the toilets, the water coolers and IT. They moan about Colin on the security desk, or Jeanie on reception. They even moan about cracks in pavements. We don't know why, but they always seem to huddle together too.

However, the group we are talking about are the Window Shoppers. That's because they are very good at talking the talk. When you meet this group of people, they'll be enthusiastic, warm and definitely into ideas. However, their forte (and we have never figured out if it's a tactic) is that they will keep you talking. Meeting after coffee, after lunch, after a beer. And when all is said and done they just keep talking, but it gets you nowhere. On a personal note, they remind us of many football managers who on paper and in their punditry talk a great talk. In reality, their actions rarely match their words and their teams suffer because of it.

So, our advice to you would be to keep your antennae twitching and watch out for this group. Treat them with a degree of caution, and eventually, if you have to, just be strong and take the necessary action. Don't worry, they won't take it personally. They will go onto the next topic soon enough.

PULLING TOGETHER ACTION-ORIENTATED PEOPLE

If you can, tune into the Passion Activists with a small representation of Resistant Fighters. These people have a desire to make a difference and the attitude to make things happen.

In Chapter 6 we talked about your sphere of influence and those of the people around you. In this section we want you to think more widely than that. If you are struggling to get things going, think about who the activists are in your organisation, beyond your department.

Rather than approaching these people with a specific innovation project, approach them as a collaborative group to solve problems, strengthening the innovation bond between you.

If there are no passion activists in your organisation, find them elsewhere. That is what great networks are about. However, remember this: make sure that the network is an active network; not just a talking network. Otherwise you will be back to square one.

THINK ACTIVE GROUP, NOT SUPPORT GROUP

There are a million and one support networks, conferences and activity groups out there. LinkedIn has specialist interest groups, which members set up for themselves. The same is true of Google, Facebook and even Twitter. They all help to establish networks of some sort.

But are they active?

A colleague of ours had an inspirational idea called 'The 500'. The idea was to pull together 500 diverse but common-minded people from all industry sectors to debate specific issues and propose solutions that they could use, promote or challenge others with. The group grew from an informal network of self-elected leaders who knew other good people with issues to share. Around 20 people came together initially. The conversations were intense, energetic and engaging. More people joined and more conversations started. The solutions the group developed were really different, but they never quite managed to implement anything. In essence it became a support group rather than an active group, even though it had some radical and attractive ideas.

The best groups we have heard of come together around an issue they are most keen on resolving. They form a type of campaign group and make sure that they understand and act together. They might be resolving issues between participants in work, or by theme or subject matter, and the support comes through doing. At first it may feel like you are investing lots of effort in extracurricular activities, but the pay-off is worth it. The benefits include:

- distance from your work environment to stand back and reflect;
- energy and ideas at times when your natural energy might be low;
- an active support network to lean on, but also to hone your skills within;
- like-minded people coming together to share stories, ideas and implementation examples, and;
- help in demonstrating the case for innovation within your organisation.

It doesn't have to be a formal group that comes together for life; think short, cyclical or moving from one issue to the next.

Some organisations have internalised this approach. They bring together people from disparate business units around common and shared interests and themes, enabling them to develop, propose and implement radical solutions. The by-product of course is the network.

dangerous quest

How do you go about setting up this type of group? Try placing an ad in your local paper, like:

'Frustrated person seeks other like-minded people to tackle local social and society problems through new and innovative thinking. Apply to...'

It's that simple. We know a person who put this style of advert in a trade magazine to attract a specific group of people. They found around 18 to 20. Others have found people through conferences, and slowly brought them together. Some have found their professional or institutional bodies more than willing to help make connections. And don't overlook friends who work in other companies. They will happily join your action group or know somebody who will.

One last tip. In the same way that you should avoid putting yourself in a position to get a no, don't get a fund together to support the group either. As soon as you do, it will fail to act. We think it's because the budget attracts people who are not necessarily in it for the right reasons. Be self-funding, or draw funds from the outcome of activities; it's an indicator of commitment and shouldn't be underestimated.

REMEMBER, IT STARTS WITH YOU, THEN THE TEAM, THEN THE ORGANISATION

If only they were different then I could be so much more creative.

There are many excuses for not starting the journey or making the step to becoming a leader. It's so easy to point the finger at anyone but yourself:

They never listen to anybody else, so why me?

And you can even point the finger back in time:

We are just too screwed up as an organisation, it needs clear leadership from the top.

We tried it 10 years ago and it didn't work then.

But when it comes down to it, it's a simple choice. You can either be a real leader, or not. Take the first step and you can make a difference, whatever the situation. It can't be any worse.

You know you want to – so leap. Now.

key learning points

- It starts with you, builds to the team...and then to the organisation. Yes, it starts with you!

- Find things that help you to make this change inevitable, desirable and linked to success.
- Build and prime the catapult that will help propel you and your leadership forward – using things that are happening already in the organisation.
- Set up a network and mutually support each other. Make it last.
- Don't wait to start. Just start.

WORD CLOUD

chapter 9
go and be the change

> 15,000 years ago, everybody was convinced the world was flat. 5,000 years ago, everybody believed the world was the centre of the universe...And five minutes ago you were convinced we were the only life in the galaxy. Now just think what you are going to learn tomorrow!

Men in Black (1997)

So here we are, the last chapter of the book. Hopefully you've been doing, as well as reading.

If you haven't thought about your core beliefs as discussed in Chapter 2, or identified how to step across your own personal line as explored in Chapter 3, then what are you doing here? Go straight to jail, don't pass go, don't collect £200, because you have missed a vital element of this book: developing you.

On the other hand, if you have done these things and maybe one or two others, then you've taken your first few important steps. Well done. Hopefully it's given you a taste to go out there and try some more.

First, let's recap a few things to help you take the next step. By the way, if you ever want a quick reminder of what we've discussed in this book, just flip to this chapter, or to the Key Learning Points and Word Clouds at the end of each chapter.

IT'S ALL ABOUT YOU

> It's all down to you; you are the change you have been waiting for.

Barack Obama

This book is about you; your beliefs, behaviours, traits as a leader and how you develop and build specific leadership, innovation and creativity capabilities to match. Hopefully you found the Innovation Leadership Wheel a great tool to help you work these out, because whilst innovation leadership has some core traits, it can also be unique to you, your challenge and your personal stretch. Our advice would be to keep that wheel on a wall somewhere, and keep referring to it. Tracking how you've grown is a great way to help keep your confidence high when times are tough.

Challenging yourself

> **Whether you think that you can, or that you can't, you are usually right.**

Henry Ford

We challenged you to think about whether, as a leader, you should be the source of creativity and innovation. We asked you to think about everyday situations that put you into your personal Stretch Zone, challenging your personal limitations and limiting beliefs about yourself and then those of your colleagues and the people around you.

We discussed the art of being a leader, the ultimate role model of creativity and innovation for others, and explained that the primary challenge for a leader is to pass on those innovation skills and capabilities. Leaders must be role models for their people, helping them to slowly push their own boundaries, behaviours and capabilities and to become more innovative and creative.

By the way, did you try all those challenges in Chapter 5 or just a few of them?

Guiding with a steady hand

> **Management is efficiency in climbing the ladder of success; leadership determines whether the ladder is leaning against the right wall.**

Stephen R Covey

When talking about you and your team, there are some key things we really want you to remember. Helping the team to be more innovative may not be just about releasing them to be more innovative in everything straight away. We think this sounds counterintuitive, but from our experience, it's about guiding the team and giving them the appropriate focus and signals, together with the right amount of permission. Coupled with recognition of their shared ambition for innovation, this will really help them to move forward quickly and purposefully. It will also protect them from blowing their confidence early.

Maintaining momentum

> **Only those who will risk going too far can possibly find out how far they can go.**

T S Eliot

Remember to light those fires. Think about and identify mini-structures that can help your team be more creative and innovative every single day. Spot them in the way you work and the routines you have. Put these in place to help guide the team and make them habitual, so they carry on even when you are not there. For example, we can guarantee that by 10 o'clock every day in our office, our team will have had a 10 minute stand-up about the progress from the day before, the learning they have uncovered, and the key activities for the day.

Remember, in those early days of getting going you still have things to deliver. All these tools help the team to do that, but you still need to be prepared to say 'Stop!' – in an appropriate way, of course.

Facilitating change

> **A pessimist sees the difficulty in every opportunity; an optimist sees the opportunity in every difficulty.**

Sir Winston Churchill

At some point you will need to think about winning other leaders round to your way of thinking. Do this by demonstrating the value of innovation, and the opportunities it creates. Some may need more convincing than others. And of course, they may have subtly different views about what type of innovation is required – their personal scale of innovation. Embrace this and help them to understand these differing viewpoints.

Don't try and do everything at once, or place your bet on just one moment. To launch, or not to launch, that is the question. Think about bringing about change in a series of waves, each wave designed to help you build energy and momentum as you go. Win over those who have the desire first and then enrol and equip them to win over others. The most effective way is to start where people are and to win them over one at a time. Each person you win over can then help you win over the next.

Think about how you use your team to seed innovation in other areas, and how you use projects and shared challenges to equip people from other teams through actual application. You may have to be prepared to fight to prevent your team, and especially its stars, from just being shuffled around in a hope that this can spread this new found capability around the organisation.

When you look across the organisation and consider how you engage people in innovation, don't fall for the traditional methods – e-mail, papers, etc. Get your creative juices going. Be nosey, be inquisitive. Find and design ways to cut through the everyday hum of the organisation, and use a variety of methods to engage people that ensure they hear you, hear your team and hear your message.

Spreading the change

> *See-feel* change is more powerful than analysis-think change.

John Kotter

How do you spread innovation around, with or without a team? How do you help people to experience it and get it into their everyday work? Go Guerrilla.

Create an underground movement that generates a desire for, as well as an expectation of, creativity and innovation in everyday life. Spot places where you can make innovation highly visible (don't forget to judge people's Comfort, Panic and Stretch Zones). Provide a taste of innovation and create the impression that innovation is a part of day-to-day living. Most of all, leave people craving more!

Get cracking – now!

> If you don't change things dramatically, you are liable to end up where you are headed.

Old proverb

And finally, the biggest lesson of all is this: don't wait, just start. Start small, start light and build to a crescendo. Find things that help you to make this change inevitable, desirable and linked to success. Find and prime the catapult to propel you and your leadership forward.

Find others outside your organisation who give you energy, confidence and help you push on – just make sure they are doers, not talkers. Set up a network and provide mutual support. Make it last.

And coming full circle, look to yourself to make it happen. As a leader, it's going to be up to you!

As somebody once said:

> **Change is inevitable — except from a vending machine.**

Anon

They say that genius is a fine line between insanity and obsession. Just look at Da Vinci, Dyson or even Darwin, who was himself shunned for trying to speak an unspeakable truth and spent over 20 years of dogged determination formulating his work into the great text. Of course, it doesn't generally take this long to make things happen.

From our experience, becoming a leader of innovation is about taking the rough with the smooth. There are forward steps and backward steps, but you will never regret it. When you have others looking up to you and asking you to be their coach or mentor, to help them be more creative or innovative, you'll know you are half way there.

Other places to draw on
As we said at the beginning, this book has chosen to not concentrate on the bigger structures for innovation and

the strategic higher ground that can help turn your whole organisation into a great innovation machine. Do not despair; below are a few little resources that can supplement your knowledge and experiences if you need them.

We have found two great online sources for company examples that can be great stimulus for you. They can be found in the innovation section of HBR Online and Business Week Online.

There is a wide variety of classic texts that you can read that explain some of the origins and thinking around the mechanics of innovation. They include, but are not limited to:

Developing Products in Half the Time, by Reinertsen
Winning at New Products, by Cooper
Understanding Organisations, by Handy
The Innovator's Dilemma, by Christensen

If you want to think about where innovation is going in the future, Von Stamm and Trifilova have published a collection of interviews from different innovators which create some interesting opinions in *The Future of Innovation*. At any rate, it will be fun to check back on this book in 10 to 15 years time to see if any of the opinions have come true.

For those wanting a little something different to add into their kit bag about engagement around the organisation (no this isn't about innovation but it has some great ideas) try *Change the World 9-5*, or, *Random Acts of Kindness*.

And of course, you can always come to our website www. impactinnovation.co.uk and this will direct you to more information about the books or additional resources you can tap into.

One final act
Before we say goodbye and good luck, there is one thing you can do for us.

final dangerous quest

Capture the story of your personal innovation journey and send it to us. It can be about your first few steps, or your first major milestone, and you don't have to wait until the end of the journey to do it. We'll publish your story online along with those of your fellow leaders for innovation. Hopefully it will become a great source of new inspiration for future leaders.

Good luck.

index